Jonathan Kahan

AN INTIMACY
WITH STILLNESS

Jonathan Kahan

AN INTIMACY
WITH STILLNESS

NADAV BOOKS

TZIVONIM
PUBLISHING

יונתן כהן
אינטימיות עם הדממה

Editors: Dr. Lea Tzivoni and Moshe Gromb

Graphic design: Ilana Lasri
Printed by Printiv, Jerusalem

Tzivonim Publishing, Tel Aviv
lea@tzivonim.com   www.tzivonim.com
Nadav Books, Kfar Saba
gromb@bezeqint.net   www.nadav-books.co.il

ISBN 978-965-548-073-3

Printed in Israel, 7/2014

Had I been born again, I would not have wished to be born in any different way.

Jonathan Kahan

Table of Contents

Editors' Introduction

A rare disease of progressive muscular dystrophy accompanied Jonathan Kahan throughout his life.

As a child he used crutches, during his youth he was in a wheelchair, and he spent most of his adult life bedridden, unable to move a limb.

The doctors predicted that he would only live for two years, but he lived a fulfilling life up to the age of sixty. During these sixty years he studied, wrote books, and found happiness and satisfaction in spite of his physical disability.

"A fully functioning body is body is not a prerequisite for happiness," Jonathan said, "Happiness belongs to whoever finds it within his self."

Two of Jonathan's books were published during his lifetime, From Damaged to Perfection – Perfection of life within a Damaged Body (1979), and Landscape of Awareness – Pictures from the Soul (1985).

Two years after Jonathan's death, additional manuscripts and chronicles by him were published in the book, The Human within Us, edited by Lea Tzivoni. This book contains a body of work that illuminates the way in which a severely disabled person consolidated his personal vision of humanity. The book contains philosophical analysis and aphorisms which suggest a new insight into human thought. The book also grants a broad view of Jonathan's life through the inclusion of photographs, illustrations and anecdotes written by his close friends and caretakers.

These friends assisted Jonathan with many aspects of his life, from mobility, access, and administrative tasks such as getting a visa for his Filipino caretaker, to University registration, writing, publishing, coordinating lectures, and taking care of household bills. He was also aided by Feldenkrais therapists who volunteered to care for him. These friends and caretakers did not only assist Jonathan, they were also themselves rewarded with personal, emotional, and intellectual enrichment. Through him they discovered how a disabled person can find happiness and fruitfulness in his life, and his courage gave them strength during difficult times in their own lives.

Now, three years after Jonathan's death, we are publishing the first collection of his manuscripts in English. These manuscripts are about the perception of human ability, concerning space, sleep, and dreams. They also serve as an indication of his human sensitivity and high cognitive skills, which enabled him to ascend to new levels of thought. In his mind he charted endless details about the universe; from his small room in North Tel Aviv he accumulated vast knowledge in philosophy (graduating with honors as a Master of Philosophy from Tel Aviv University) as well as Art, Music, Literature and Science, which all together created his broad world.

Reading An Intimacy with Stillness is a moving experience, allowing the reader to become acquainted with the magical life that existed within the mind of a physically disabled person. It offers a deep philosophical outlook and insight into humanity. This book was prepared for editing by Jonathan himself, but he unfortunately passed away and was unable to see the task completed. The manuscripts are published in his style and language, and not edited or corrected to avoid repetitions. Jonathan had a commendable grasp of English thanks to his familial background, and so we did not attempt to improve or change his wording to adhere to any rules of political correctness. Thus, for example, Jonathan writes of being "crippled" rather than being "disabled". That is his style and his message to the world.

Many of Jonathan's manuscripts are yet to be published, but all of them carry a message – they offer compassion and grant hope. In this book the reader is invited to join Jonathan on his sixty year journey and witness his insights regarding life.

Moshe Gromb and **Dr. Lea Tzivoni**
Editors

A MAN-MADE DESTINY

All my life I have had a drive and tendency to think about things of consequence. I remember myself as being deeply inclined towards abstract thinking, but only superficially concerned with concrete action. It did not occur to me that abstract thinking made me forget and ignore the bodily handicap I have as a cripple. Neither did it occur to me that by reflecting upon my physical problem, I could revolutionize the notions I had about myself and about life.

My condition is what is medically referred to as "Progressive Muscular Dystrophy". As it implies, it is a progressive wasting away of the muscles and, as a result, an ever increasing incapacity in bodily movement. An ordinary person will develop his physique during the first 5 years of life. However, my body became less and less powerful with the passing of each phase of my first 25 years. Naturally, as a consequence, my adversity was a major factor in directing the events of my life. Since my very first years, and up till

Jonathan was born on 27 October 1951, a normal baby. He developed and started to crawl, but could not stand on his legs. When he was less than one year old his mother felt that something was wrong with him. A physician checked and found out that Jonathan did not respond. They went to see a neurologist and he diagnosed his disease and told them he would not live more than two and a half years.

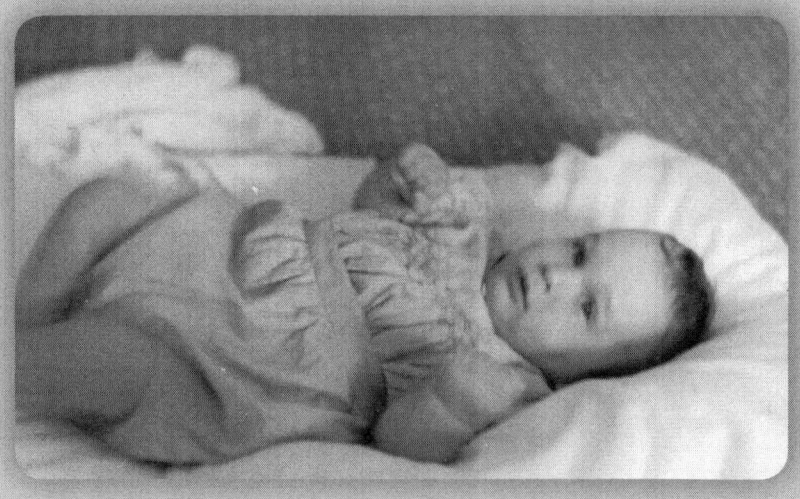

Jonathan baby, London 1952

today, my world has revolved around a central change in proportion between paralysis and movement. The more my activities matured and became complex, the more did my growing sickness force me to rely upon those around me. My darling mother made sure I would be taken for outings. My movements might be restricted, but she wanted to ensure I would not lack for mobility.

As a child, I was still able, using my own strength, to move my body physically from place to place. Owing to this state of affairs a vitally important understanding stayed implanted in my memory. In those distant days I realized that even though I could always move my body when I wanted to, bodily movement in itself could never elevate my spirit. Another discovery of those days was that whenever deciding not to move my body, I lost nothing of my sense of well-being. Thus, even as my physical condition grew weaker, I, at no time, felt that I could not do without the experience of bodily movement. Therefore, my malady was not a process which made me feel miserable. My inner senses, my heart, whatever, told me that from every stage of my sickness I would make something creative. This something would not be an obstacle to everyday life, but would develop and deepen it.

As dystrophy progressed, I observed how my life was successfully acclimatizing itself to its changing existence. I had a strong feeling that each further stage of incapacity was harmoniously adapting itself to my day-to-day activities. Each additional waning of my strength had found its setting quite naturally in my behavioral pattern. This personal impression of what was happening to me

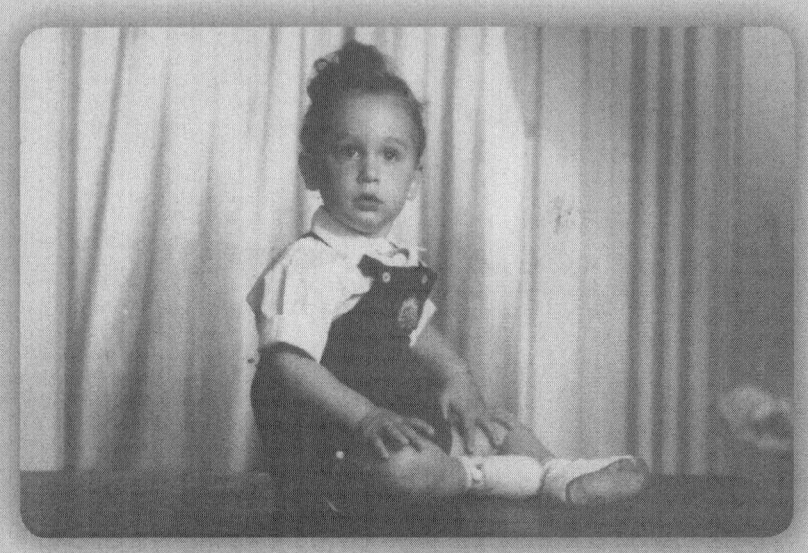

A normal baby

Jonathan and his mother

made me more acutely aware of the transition from phase to phase of my inability. I became sensitive to the meaning of living, as my existence was going through a continuous transformation of the body.

I felt that the more I sought to understand the particularism of my body, the more original would be my inclination to discover myself. What was more, I would not let myself relate in a negative way to my crippled physique before I had learnt to establish my attitude towards it. Guided by those instincts, I set out to minutely investigate the mysteries life held for a body such as mine. I used my self-awareness as a sort of "research laboratory", wherein I collated all data concerning the changes incapacity produced within me. Whenever I reached a new phase of muscular dystrophy, I sought out its effects and implications upon my life. Then I compared them, by the same yardstick, to my life in a former bodily condition. Once I had discovered the compensations in my present status, my instincts guided me to resign myself to the given condition by reconciling myself to it.

As an author, I intend writing little about myself because in this book, I can learn to know myself only indirectly. I find out about myself through studying adversity. This book says a lot on the subject of adversity, for I can study it directly from the source – myself.

My malady – the course of my being in a wheelchair – confined in early life and later confined to bed. At this point I can only speak and move my eyes. The paradox: I sense today that my being severely disabled is the fact that has contributed most to the development of the life I

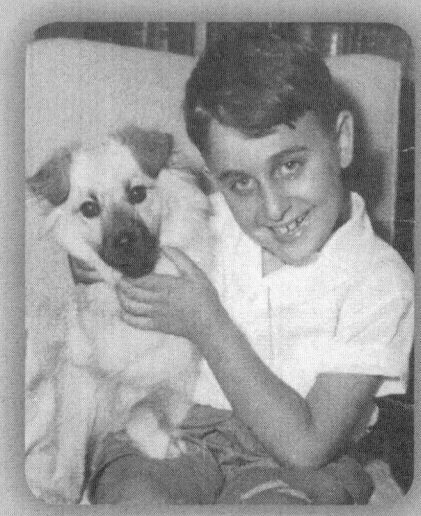

Jonathan 8 years old. 1959

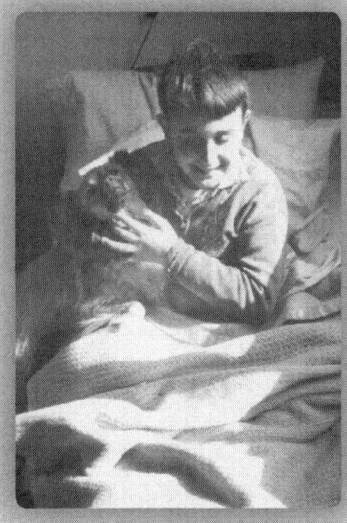

Jonathan 10 years old, 1961

Jonathan 9 years old, 1960

have lived. I sense my malady as something that has been an enormously constructive factor. Had I been born again, I would not have wished to be born in any different way.

My present day attitude to disability began in my mid-twenties. I then felt for the first time a sense of ignorance concerning my malady. I then decided to adopt a new attitude towards paralysis – a decision to look into my condition, investigate it, explore and know more about it.

What I found in my malady was very different than what one could expect. Instead of finding anything that had to do with a lack of health, what emerged before me was a profound sense of stillness contained within my paralyzed bones and muscles. I discovered an abundance of quietude in my organism as it lay motionless on my bed.

I will try to explain what I mean by "quietude". I think that most people have a sense of peacefulness that exists everywhere in nature. I believe most people find some beauty in the stillness of trees, mountains or of a sunset.

From my own point of view, being disabled as I am, I believe that the stillness that people find in the world around them or inside themselves is only the "tip of the iceberg". My personal experience would testify that the stillness accessible to a human being is far greater and more powerful than the beauty of a tree, a mountain or a sunset. I intend in these pages to describe those sensations of beauty that I have known when encountering the immobility of my own system.

In what follows I intend to present my physical state not as a shortcoming, but quite the opposite. I would like it to serve the reader in order to explore, within his or her own life, some new regions of exceptional meaning, which

Jonathan 14 years old, 1965

Jonathan 11 years old, 1962

I believe every single person has. My belief is that my paralysis can serve such a purpose and I want to write this book with this purpose in mind.

Being disabled or paralyzed is a condition that one sees more and more with the development of modern societies. On the one hand, there are more and more means of rehabilitating people, at least to some degree. On the other hand, however, with the development of our technological means, it seems that inevitably more and more accidents occur and thus there are more and more disabled people. A hundred years ago there were no car crashes, since there were no cars and thus no victims of such accidents. There is a good chance that in the future people will risk new dangers with ever more technological advancements of which we have no inkling yet. When working with my paralysis and profiting from it, I had the sense that not only could it become a physical advantage; I had the sense that in some strange way the investigation into disability goes hand in hand with the overall advancements of modern life. My hope is that understanding disability can indeed become the "high-tech" in understanding human life in general.

My situation and capabilities within that reality in which I live – my philosophy gives expression to whatever I have discovered for myself from the circumstances of my life. In fact, the only right I can claim for undertaking to explain the subject is my life, which has been lived under those very circumstances to which I relate. Because of it, I have no preconceived ideas or prejudices, and my experience can but serve as the linchpin upon which to balance my

Jonathan learned at Tkuma School for Disabled behind Carmel Market. This school was built in the 1950s following the polio epidemic which affected many children. They would bring him to school and return him. During those years he used crutches. He ate by himself with certain restrictions. In highschool he used a wheelchair.

I was Yonatan's homeroom teacher in Grades 7 and 8. Yonatan was a very special child. He had extensive knowledge of all subjects; he was very active in the lessons and always contributed to them. Yonatan was calm, quiet and very polite. The other children both loved and appreciated him and his knowledge. He was also socially active and used to meet with the other children at home. He never took advantage of the fact that he was disabled and always completed all of the required assignments. There was a period when he had to stay home for a long time, so they installed a system in his home that connected him to the classroom. He heard the teachers and saw the pupils and in this way was able to participate in the lesson in an active manner. I remember Yonatan as an excellent pupil and a very nice boy.

Vered Wexler

judgment of reality. The starting point of my search was a wish to find out systematically my situation and capabilities within that reality in which I lived. If my lot was to live as a cripple, then I was born without that knowledge I needed to live the life I had been born to. Yet I did not want my life to pass without understanding whatever activity, function or personal fulfillment that incapacity could permit.

I believe little has been done to seriously research the meaning of life for the invalid, the cripple. I cannot overcome the impression that very few people have any cognizance of the cripple's hidden resources. We shall become more acquainted with those resources later on. Thus, rather than leave the situation as I have found it, I determined to write a methodical description which could become the framework for intellectual study of a more penetrating understanding of the cripple's life.

All of us can understand that invalidism is a given situation. It exists as part and parcel of modern society. To most, if not to all, it is explained in general terms as an incurable tragedy. To the individual it is a terrible fate. I, personally, am of the opinion that the enormous gravity of the situation requires us to give a much more dialectical appraisal of the subject in place of, what at best are, shallow views. True it is that most believe physical limitations are difficult to live with, harsh and oppressive. Yet contrary to that belief, as I shall explain later on, the difficulties, the harshness, the oppression – are applicable only to the physical body.

Even in these modern times, how a cripple lives is a puzzle to most. People wonder how, for some, life is fuller and more meaningful than it is for many ordinary, normal

Jonathan (center) with his classmates at Tkuma School, 1959

people. To achieve it, the cripple must gain a definite advantage in precisely that sphere that is most important to man, namely an independent, active body, despite his obvious disadvantages. This does not come about in spite of their condition, but because of it, and as a result of it. The surprising aspect of it is the extent of their successes in accomplishing what they anticipated out of life.

An ordinary, healthy human being trains his body to walk, to run, jump, dance, ride a bicycle, fly an airplane, and so forth. Hence, he can do a variety of things, not one of which is within the scope of the cripple. Naturally, to a healthy person these functions are simply the outcome of his capability of movement, which the normal body possesses.

Every cripple learns about human capabilities through a distorted physical body. Incapacity is an inflexible condition to him. Thus, incapacity gives him a new, permanent factor with which he must cope in the correct manner. In order to do this on a permanent basis, he must develop his actions from the physical restrictions at his disposal. He must create a veritable upheaval in his attitude towards life; for only by so doing can he discover the usage of his incapacity, and his ability to activate it as raw material, opening up new vistas, new spheres of life. The challenge, of course, is to learn how to manipulate one's incapacity, and how to provide the crippled body with actions and activities which originate with the cripple himself. Seen from that viewpoint, paralysis supplies the cripple with the potential for directing his incapacity into practical channels.

Because, dear reader, maby you are not a cripple, you are normal, healthy body is a permanent factor in your life.

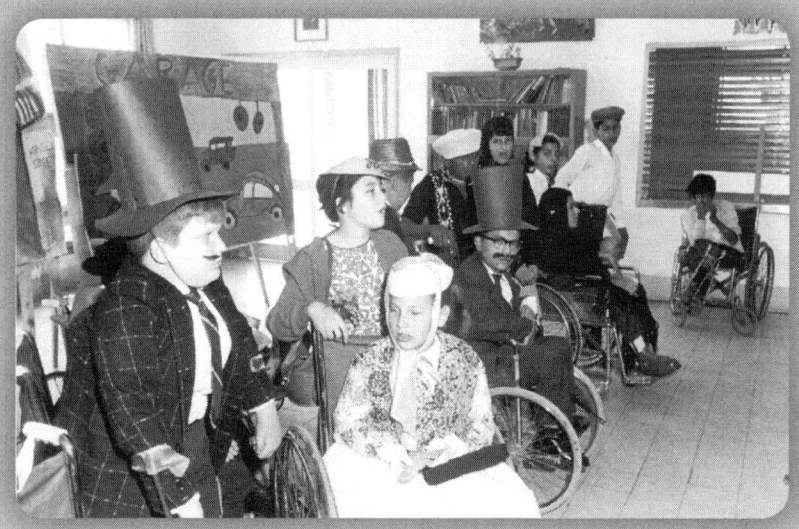

Purim at Tkuma School

Independence Day at Tkuma School.

Thus, it is the permanent factor directing your physical life and, as such, is completely different from any physical or bodily factor which incapacity has created in my life. Hence, the life I, as a cripple, am capable of developing, is completely different from the world which opens up before you. Probably I never shall see that world that is yours; and just as probably, you will never see my world. However, it is just because of that that weight is added to the need for communication between our worlds. It would open up both of our worlds to new resources which I, perhaps, could never draw upon from my world, or you from yours. My purpose in writing this book is to create a media of communication between my world of cripples and your ordinary world; to bring to you, dear reader, a message from an unusual world from your vantage point, from a world you know nothing about. The message I convey to you in this book is intended to give you a realistic concept of life in my world.

Childhood Drawings

CHAPTER 1

AN OUTLINE

In view of my malady's contribution and the striking contrast between this contribution and different phases of paralysis in my life, I wish to describe these phases.

This new attitude challenges all attempts to overcome the malady – hide it, conceal it and adopt the prevailing rehabilitation methods. Thus I turn myself into a "guinea pig" using my life as a test-tube: using the fact that I am confined to a bed and wheelchair as a means of discovering more about life.

The investigation produces a new set of experiences and I find myself living in a new world, paralysis introducing the world to me as an unknown planet.

I define a new planet – a new sense of light, space, air and gravitation. The feeling is that an encounter with disability is almost like an encounter with an extra-terrestrial form of life, a sensation of involvement that resembles science fiction, like travelling to another part of the cosmos.

Childhood Drawings

I explored my disability through taking walks in my wheelchair to a natural resort near my house. I felt on these occasions that an investigation into my stillness was also an investigation into the stillness of the trees, the riverbed, the nearby running river, the stillness of the sky above, and the stillness of the earth below.

Each person has a skull and a skeleton which, unless fractured, remains still. I felt that investigating disability was equal to an investigation of the general presence of stillness in each and every individual.

As I was doing this, I had a feeling that until then my life had been caught up in the habit of over-appreciating movement and under-appreciating stillness. I discovered within myself a sort of blindness about the value of inertia and the role it played in human life. This distorted the perspective I had of non-movement and non-performance.

The thought occurred to me – how come that one accepts a bouquet or even a single flower as a token of happiness, celebration and blessing. Flowers cannot do anything nor can they perform through movement. They cannot wave their leaves, they cannot move their petals nor can they act upon anything by using their stem. It occurred to me that in this sense one could assess flowers as being "paralyzed" or even "disabled". Flowers are rooted in the soil of their growth in a way that reminded me of being confined to an unchanging place – either my bed or the seat of my wheelchair. However, being bed- or wheelchair-confined was regarded by me until then as almost a disaster. How come then, I ask myself again, that I did not consider the condition of a flower a disaster? Why did a bouquet

Jonathan's father Sydney Kahan was born in England in 1913. In World War II he served in the British army. He Was the deputy of Haim Herzog when Bergen-Belsen was Liberated. During the War of Independence he came to Israel and joined the IDF. After the war in 1949 he returned to England.

Jonathan's mother Anna was born in Russia in 1920. Her grandfather invented and patented the railroad tracks on the Trans-Siberian Railway and built a factory that made him one of the wealthiest men in Kiev. Her Father Abraham was appointed director of the company. In 1923 her parents left their home with her and her sister Elisabeth and came to Berlin. A year later they left for Paris. After her Father died, her mother ran the restaurant, which her mother (Anna's mother) had opened, called Tel-Aviv. They lived in poverty. In 1940 the Germans invaded France, and the family fled to the south. During the war they wandered from village to village. In 1944-1945 Anna joined the Haganah and ran the illegal immigrant transit camp at Marseilles. In 1949 she visited the country of Israel and returned to France.

symbolize an abundance of happiness and life? Could I learn from flowers that being inert in almost every possible way could result in ultimate beauty – a beauty so great that it exists beyond words?

The thought occurred to me that each flower must have an extraordinary capacity. It knows how to bring together many still elements, the immobility of the earth, of its stem, of its roots, leaves and petals – and to produce something that is far more than a heap of sheer rubble or waste. Through accumulating so many such unmoving elements, it knows how to bring about a great wonder, the splendor or blossoming. I was toying with the thought that there must exist many thousands of different kinds of flowers, each of which knows how to transform its own characteristic inert elements (its special leaves, petals, stems, etc.) into a unique way of blossoming. In short, I concluded in my mind that flowers possess a great knowledge which I, as a disabled person, realized I did not have. Like most of the plant world, I too possessed a large accumulation of still elements – my still limbs, still bones and still muscles. However, I had failed thus far to produce a new far-reaching meaning. I felt a need to try and grasp that wisdom which every single plant around me seemed to exhibit. I wanted to become at least as intelligent as a plant.

After having looked into the world of flowers and trees, an even more disturbing thought occurred to me. What about the earth, the hills or a mountain? All of them are nothing more than sheer minerals. The earth displays great stillness – unless stricken by an earthquake. A mountain

Anna and Sydney, London 1957

Anna and Sydney met on the ship that departed from Haifa. They married in 1949 and lived in London. In 1953 they immigrated to Israel and lived at 14 Renanim Street, Ramat Gan. Sydney was a chemist at the Defense Ministry. Then he worked at the nuclear reactor at Nahal Sorek. Anna worked at Zim. They divorced in 1960. Jonathan was 9. Anna married Arie Munitz.

performs even greater marvels than the earth – the Himalaya's grandeur seems to attract tourists the world over. People are willing to travel great distances only to witness this outstanding power. Nature seems to know how to extract this overwhelming sense of majesty from a mere amalgamation of minerals. Seen from this perspective, minerals appeared to possess an essential knowledge which I had not yet discovered in my inert system.

When I first observed my physical condition, I could certainly find disability present throughout the whole of my system. Clearly, most of my muscles could not move nor could most of my joints and bones. In short, one could say that I made a discovery – I discovered how disabled I was. However, no matter how much I tried to find within the condition of my system a potential through which I could further my life – I again and again failed to find or discover such a potential. It seemed to me that such a potential simply did not exist. Disability was a dead-end which led nowhere rather than a main street that would lead one to many new destinations. Thus for as long as I was seeking for a latent potential in my condition, that would allow me to reach other domains than the ones I already knew I found no way out. I was locked in my condition, and being locked in it was the only discovery I could make about it. What introduced a major change in my way of life was the attempt to create or invent a new way of using disability rather than trying to discover something old that existed in it. This new approach was about using disability as a means of creating a new potential in my life. Let me try to clarify the issue of producing the potential of disability,

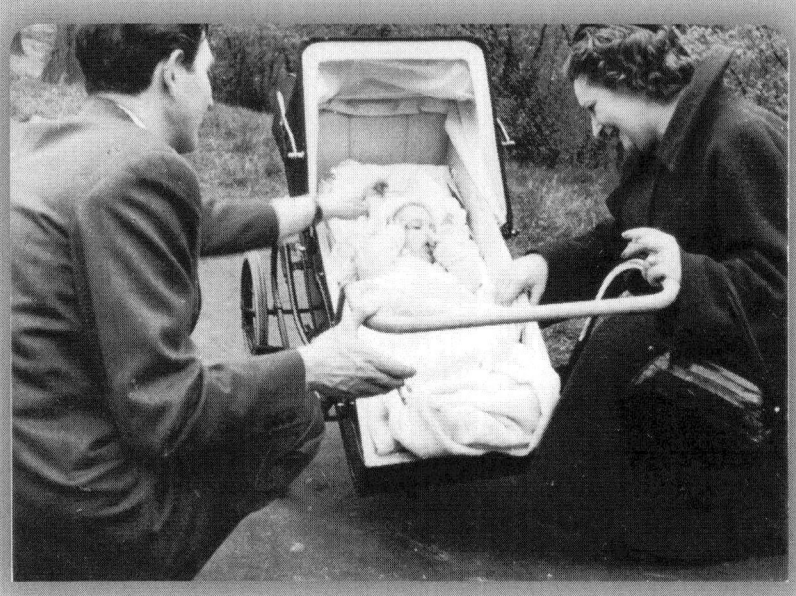

Anna and Sydney with baby Jonathan in London, 1951

Jerusalem, 1962

rather than discovering this potential. In order to explain the difference between what I mean by "producing" and "discovering", one could say that whereas Columbus discovered America, some other people thousands of years before Columbus must have invented the raft, the boat and finally the ship. What is relevant to disability is not the discovery of America but the invention of the raft (it was always there) and therefore it could be discovered by Columbus. However the potential of disability is not part of the world, has never been a part of the world and will never be a part of the world unless people invent it. The potential of disability cannot be discovered. Instead, just like a raft or the "Santa Maria", through disability one could produce, in an artificial way, a potential that never existed in a natural way. That is, one could artificially create this potential, thus bringing into being the as yet non-existent presence of a new type of disability. This new model of disability would be a type of physical paralysis which had a potential. This new brand of a handicap would serve as an instrument, which could be used in a variety of new ways. The "Santa Maria" had just such an artificial potential – to sail either to India or America or any other new continent on the face of the globe. This potential, made available by the ship, was completely artificial and man-made. Not one ship – not the "Santa Maria", the "Mayflower", nor even the "Titanic" grew on trees – nor were they harvested in any field. All of these vessels have the potential of sailing just because they were man-made and thus designed to have this potential. I would like to introduce a more modern (and thus more updated) analogy to the way in which I approached my condition. Since the middle of the

Arie Munitz was born in Lithuania in 1912. His father was killed in World War I. His mother remarried and had three more sons. As a child he helped support the family. In the Betar Movement he was introduced to Zionism and to the theory of Jabotinsky. In 1936 he obtained a certificate from the Hebrew University and immigrated to Israel. His family was murdered in the Holocaust of European Jewry. He married Sarah Hanoch, and they had two daughters, Shlomit and Esther. Arie lived in Jerusalem, studied humanities at the Hebrew University and was active in the Irgun. Later he finished his law studies and was a legal advisor to the city of Ramat Gan. He volunteered in Rotary and the Freemasons. After his wife passed away he married Anna. He was crippled, he had deformed hand. He supported Jonathan and helped him as much as he could. Arie passed away in 1997.

In the sixties Anna and Arie bought two ground floor apartments in a building at 19 Bnei Moshe Street and joined them together. The northern entrance went directy to Jonathan's room. The south had two entrance doors from the stair well, the west door to the kitchen and in the east to Anna's residence.

Arie Munitz and daughters Shlomit
and Etty

20th century, most people would agree that mankind had the potential of going to the moon. Two hundred years ago, only lunatics would have believed such a thing. What changed the attitude of people between 1750 and 1950? Certainly, the moon itself remained exactly as it was during those 200 years. Why did people in 1950 believe that the moon was accessible whilst their ancestors in 1750 believed it to be inaccessible? The moon itself remained as yellow and round as it had always been. The difference between those two historical eras was that only in the 20th century did mankind invent and produce both astronauts and the space shuttle. Strangely enough, the potential of mankind to go to the moon was not brought about by the moon's presence, but rather by the presence of astronauts and space shuttles. Coming back to the issue of disability- as long as I was thinking of a potential I could discover through studying the nature of the "moon" (that is, a potential I could discover by studying the nature of disability itself) I could only fail time and again, and regard all such attempts as "lunatic". It was only when I turned to the production of an "astronaut" (who could travel in a "space shuttle") that my attempt began to make sense. What was required was to invent a new concept of mankind and of what a human being is. Just like in the case of space travel – no one could conceive of an 'astronaut' before such a thing existed (was artificially invented) – the same also held true of disability. What was required was to invent a new way of using paralyzed muscles, bones and joints, thus creating a new human entity and a new way in which to live human life.

New Reality

Yonatan was my brother – in fate and in life. Fate brought us both together at a dramatic crossroads. I experienced a painful separation from my mother, who had died at a young age, leaving my father, my sister Eti, and myself abandoned and broken. For Yonatan the breaking up of his small family framework left him heartbroken. My father and his mother decided to befriend one another, taking with them, us – the children – to another reality, not of our own choosing.

Shlomit Munitz-Rib

An Anomaly

I met you when you were six years old. You were in a wheelchair. A smart boy, very polite, an only child of parents who completely dedicated themselves to your treatment and support. We were forced to move to a new home, where we now supposedly lived together, but each of us lived a separate life – one from the other.

Anna dedicated herself to Yonatan's care, worried about his physical needs, and opened up cultural and social worlds for his benefit. My father found solace in his public work away from home, and in his hobby – stamp collecting. Endowed with the traits of compassion, empathy and honesty, he entered this new life with full awareness.

This sense of anomaly pervaded everything. It was a complicated, complex household, from both a physical and emotional point of view. Life went on, and each participant found his own way to survive within this complex reality.

Shlomit Munitz-Rib

This new brand of disability – which must first be invented for it to exist at all – would have to be different from what exists now, in that the new invented type must serve as an instrument. Paralysis, instead of existing as an unavoidable given condition, should, I suggest, serve as a means of achieving specific aims.

At this point, we need to be clear about the terms "means" and "aims" as they are used here. To clarify the point, I will compare the invented brand of paralysis with certain organs of our biological make-up. The human eye can be considered as an organ that reveals the visual aspect of the world to us. Our eyes show us the colors of the world, its shapes, light shadows, and so on. When we consider our eyes in this way, it is important to emphasize that the world has its own colors, shapes, light and shadows, and all the rest, regardless of whether we see them or not. Had we no eyes, we would not see the world, but it does not follow from this that the world would have lost its colors, shapes and all the rest. The sun, we may assume, would be as glowing as it is, the sky would be as blue even if we couldn't see them.

Our eyes, however, do not only reveal to us the visual aspects of the world; they also disclose to us the colors of movies, the shapes of letters, the fit of clothes, and a long series of other visual stimuli, which our eyes are trained to observe. Our eyes were not born as reading instruments, but were made to become so through the invention of letters, printing and even spectacles. An illiterate person looking at a printed page would not know what letters look like or identify a word or a sentence.

Jonathan and his mother, 1979

A Wonderful Woman

This beautiful woman, Annie, she made him what he was. All of his moral and cultural values – he learned them from her. What an amazing woman. And together with all this, she really was extremely beautiful. She always answered the door with a radiant smile.

Mia Segal

The French teacher

Yonatan and I met by chance when I was studying French with his wonderful mother, Annie. Annie introduced us when she understood, with her special sensitivity, that I would find such a friendship interesting. And that's exactly how it was.

Ilan Eshed

In short, reading eyes are organs that was invented and produced by mankind. The same may be said of eyes that follow the development of a movie on a screen. To take these examples a step further, let us consider eyes that look through a telescope and see the universe as it was half a billion years ago: that is, eyes trained to observe distances of half a billion light years away. Such eyes would reveal to us not only the colorful aspects of the world and its shapes and shades, but also the spatial dimensions of the cosmos itself. Now let us return to our original comparison: The analogy between the way in which our sight works and the way in which paralysis can be put to use. The invented model of disability that I have in mind could be used as an instrument to reveal a hitherto almost unknown aspect of the world. I believe that disabled muscles, joints and bones, if trained to become an organ that I believe they can become, would serve to detect the stillness of the world. This new organ, made of paralyzed tissues, would reveal to us the still aspect of reality in a way which we have, I believe, never known. In what follows I intend to describe and analyze this stillness in the way I experienced it when it was revealed to me through a use of my disabled system. As I viewed the world through my paralysis it seemed to expose new aspects of its own stillness, aspects to which I was completely "blind" until I began using my paralysis to unravel them.

As I observed these aspects of stillness it was very obvious to me that they belonged to the world in any case – whether I acknowledged them or ignored them (as I believe most of humanity does). I realized that the world itself has always held and probably always will hold

Optimism

Over the past years, since my sister Etti as well as my father have passed on, I became very close to Annie and Yonatan. I got to know both him and his mother. I learned to respect and appreciate her wisdom. I admired the Zionist activities she had engaged in during WWII, and especially her endless dedication to Yonatan. The optimism that flowed from Yonatan never ceased to amaze me. In our phone conversations and during my visits with him, I always experienced encouragement, interest and true support.

Shlomit Munitz-Rib

Childhood

Jonathan's childhood was a long path of gradual discovery, gradual understanding and internalization of his physical attributes, while building himself up: building up the strength which enabled him, and pushed him to spread his wings.

It happened under the cover of a normal life which we, those surrounding him – his mother first and foremost, who sustained most of the effort – attempted to create.

We surrounded him, but he steeled himself on his own, in the depth of his soul, in absolute secrecy. That was the secret he has kept within himself ever since, evolving throughout Jonathan's life, and which marked his approach until his final day.

during his childhood, he took the shock in step by step, concealed his reactions, and internally constructed, within himself, the incomprehensible moral strength which all of us admired afterwards.

It all transpired before my eyes, but I failed to understand.

stillness which is far more profound and elaborate than most people have ever envisioned. This stillness has never been available to us because we have not trained ourselves to be attentive to it. Disability, if used as an instrument, can serve such a purpose: it can allow us to encounter this complete aspect of reality that has remained outside the range of our experience.

Let us consider another example of a human organ which through being trained can reveal an ever broadening aspect of the world. The human brain when trained to think mathematically can reveal the physical, chemical and biological laws that prevail in nature. What our brain discovers is that the world is governed by mathematical principles. Even when we do not analyze the world mathematically we assume that its workings must follow mathematical principles. The world is ruled by the laws of mathematics even when we ignore these laws. However, the more the natural sciences make progress the more accessible to us does the source of mathematical laws become. When our brain is equipped with the adequate physical, chemical and biological knowledge, the world which we then observe will yield an abundance of further mathematical insights and rules. My feeling is that paralysis, when regarded as an organ that can be trained to detect the stillness of reality, can act according to the same rule. The more paralysis will have made progress in exposing the unknown stillness of the world, the more additional resources of stillness will the world reveal to it. My own personal experience as a disabled person had already shown me that the depth of stillness which awaits

When I made aliya with my mother – the only sister of Jonathan's mother – about a year after Jonathan and his parents, he and I used to spend our Sabbaths together playing, mainly with toy soldiers and other lead or plastic figures. But more than we played, we talked: he asked questions and I answered them (I was his elder by almost five years). Rarely and anxiously, and in extreme situations, he would ask me questions indirectly related to physical handicaps – always on a general and unspecific level. This was when nobody had yet talked to him about his situation openly. As soon as he began studying in Abrams elementary school, there was a breakthrough and the subject of the handicap ceased to be taboo.

Allon Lev

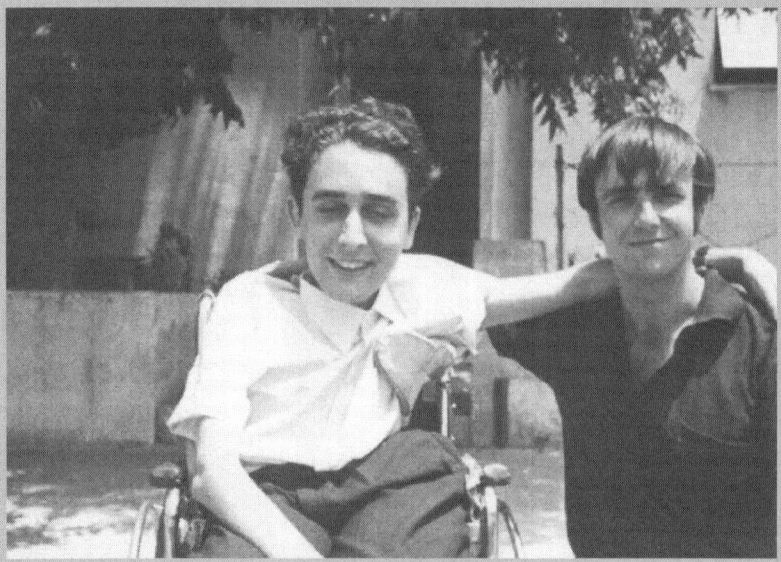

Allon and Jonathan

us in the very core of reality seems to be almost unlimited. We have so far ignored an almost endless abundance of stillness which could become available to us deep in the presence of the world around us.

In order to clarify this notion I applied a metaphor. I likened our "natural" biological traits to the ingredients needed for preparing a dish. Very few people would want to consume most of these ingredients – flour, salt, sugar or a raw egg. Thus there exists a striking contrast between the ingredients that are used to prepare a dish and the "end-product" that one would want to eat. The initial ingredients would need to be chopped, spiced, boiled, fried or baked in order for them to become a delectable dish. This resulting "final product" would bear little resemblance to the "raw materials" from which it was made.

With this notion clear in mind I ask myself whether all our natural biological "resources" were being put to use. In other words, did we possess some additional biological traits that still existed in us as "raw material", without us, thus far, having discovered a way of cultivating them. At first glance almost all our biological resources seemed to have been exhausted. I had already recognized the various ways in which sight, thinking and movement have been humanly remolded. I could equally trace back the transformation of a myriad of other natural "processes" – hearing (in speech, music, etc.) taste (through the development of a variety of different cuisines) and even clothing (clothes and even haute couture replacing animal skins or furs in maintaining the body's temperature).

Dr. Moshe Feldenkrais was the first person I met who was able to answer all my questions willingly and give reliable non evasive answers

Jonathan Kahan

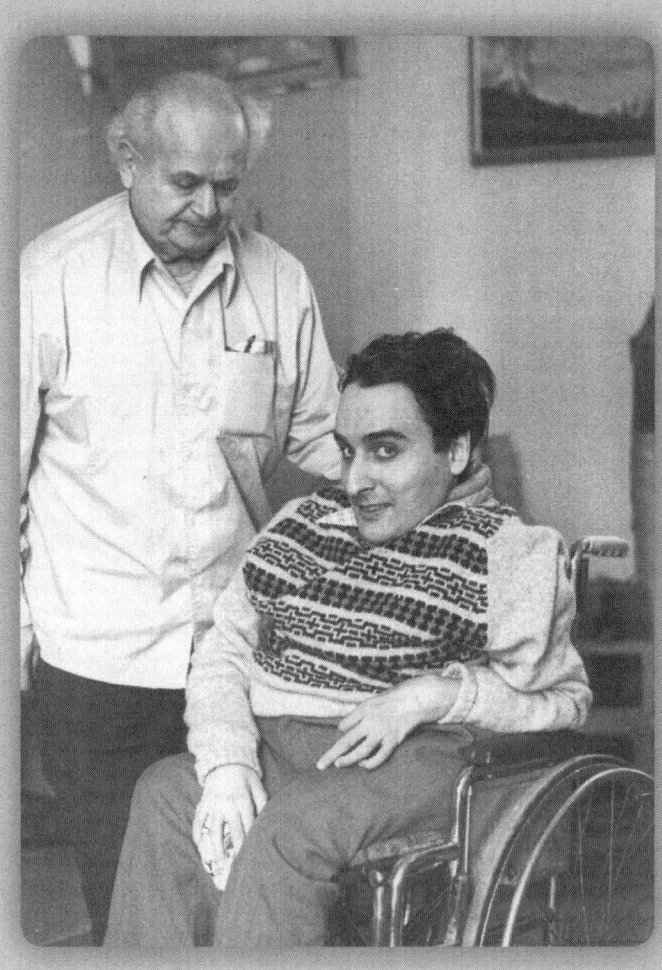

Jonathan and Dr. Moshe Feldenkrais

I felt that a search was taking place within me – I was exploring my own life, looking for a biological aspect that was present in me in its "raw" condition. Then suddenly, I was struck by a new sensation. I experienced, for the first time, the paralysis of my system as a "raw material". All at once I no longer felt my immobility as the "end product" of my malady. The question arose: what if through using my paralyzed bones in some innovative way I could plan a hitherto unknown form of life. Can I address my disability as an aspect of myself which could reveal as yet un-thought-of potentials? Could I consider my inertia as the ingredients of an as yet unknown dish which I will season, spice, chop, boil, fry or bake in order to produce in the world completely new flavours.

I can undertake such a project only if I equip myself with several working assumptions that will serve as guides on this journey.

The first assumption is that I will be using paralyzed muscles, disabled joints and immobile bones. In the "cooking" metaphor these would be the ingredients from which I intend to prepare my "dish". They have in their raw state little or no flavor. The worthlessness of my inert body-parts would be analogous to salt, flour, and raw eggs which most people find completely dull and unappetizing. Similarly my muscles, joints and bones are certainly a part of my life and as such they evidently exist, but only in a way that has very little value for me.

When I look inwards into my own system I can find no trace of the potential which I am looking for. What I find in my system are the motionless muscles, bones and joints

I cannot help

I know that in the beginning Feldenkrais told Annie that he didn't think he could help, but Annie asked him again when Yonatan was eight or nine years old, and then they began working with him.

Lior Pessach

Jonathan and Dr. Moshe Feldenkrais

but these bear no witness to any potential that lies beyond them. The "dish" metaphor would explain this: one could search into a raw egg for as long as one liked, one could study the nature of flour or observe all the different aspects of salt. Even the most thorough study of these ingredients would not yield the faintest sign of, say, a baked cake. Were one to expect to find a baked cake in salt, in flour or in a raw egg one would conclude that such a thing as a baked cake simply does not exist. Indeed nowhere in the world can a baked cake be found. The only way to find a baked cake is to bake it. Being disabled I felt that the same held true of the potential of disability. One needed to "bake" it for it to be present at all in the world. The potential I was in search of could only be the result of my own endeavor to produce it. In principle producing this potential would be the only way which would allow it to exist.

I assume that the "recipe" for developing disability can only be found in "recipe books" – it cannot be found in the world of nature where everything is uncooked. Thus the recipe for the cooking of disability into its becoming a new dish should be written in terms that are as general as possible. Being a recipe it must be understandable by any reader who wants to follow the instructions. Any reader should be able to open the book, read the "recipe" and "cook" the same ingredients in that person's own "kitchen". The potential of disability must belong not only to my own system, but rather should be relevant to the life of any other reader of "recipe books" who wants to do his own cooking. In other words what I intend my paralyzed body to undergo in order to develop itself, should become a process which anyone can use and reuse with any other inert system.

Just his head

When I first visited him in 1960, I didn't even know why I was coming.

Moshe Feldenkrais said: "Look, I'm treating a boy; he's got this and that, come and see what I'm doing with him."

When I entered the house, I didn't know what I was getting into. The boy sat there in his chair and, in the first moment I didn't expect it because his body was small and his head was big, and his eyes… Suddenly I didn't know where I was; it was so moving to see only his head. Within maybe two minutes, as soon as he began to speak, you immediately forgot that he wasn't one of us, wasn't like us. Afterwards we went into his room, and there were toys, a train and soldiers, like all the children. Everything was neat and tidy. They had a very difficult life. I began working with him and this went on for a long time – 15 years, until I left to travel in Japan.

Mia Segal

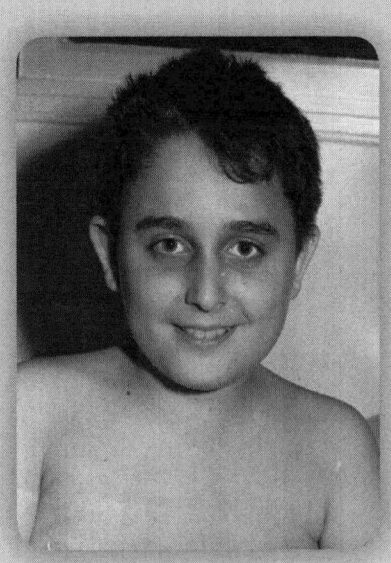

Feldenkrais exercises

Another assumption is that the potential I am trying to develop through my paralysis can be of a physical nature only. In other words, the nature of this potential cannot be either mental or spiritual. The "baked cake" metaphor can again clarify this point. The ingredients that go into a cake (or for that matter into any dish) are all of a material nature. Flour, salt and a raw egg exist physically in the world of matter.

The "end product" of such "raw materials" is as material as the ingredients. A cake, however delectable the chef made it, can never be a mental product – it is as physical as the oven in which it has been baked. My inert bones can be likened to the salt in my metaphor, my paralyzed muscles to the flour and my disabled joints can be represented by a raw egg. If this analogy is carried further, the potential of my condition can be compared to a cake that has already been baked. The enterprise that awaits me as a disabled person can be symbolized by the baking of a cake – a project carried out in its entirety, through matter alone.

I assume that in order to develop the potential of disability one needs an environment that can be instrumental to this purpose. The "cooking" metaphor would provide such an environment – a kitchen with refrigerator and stove. The kitchen as a whole would provide an environment for the transformation of the ingredients (the raw materials) into a baked cake (the end product). The refrigerator would be an environment for storing the ingredients (eggs, milk) whilst the stove would be a different environment serving a different purpose – an environment without which no baking or frying could take place. For the process of transforming the ingredients into a baked cake all three environments (kitchen, refrigerator and stove) are required.

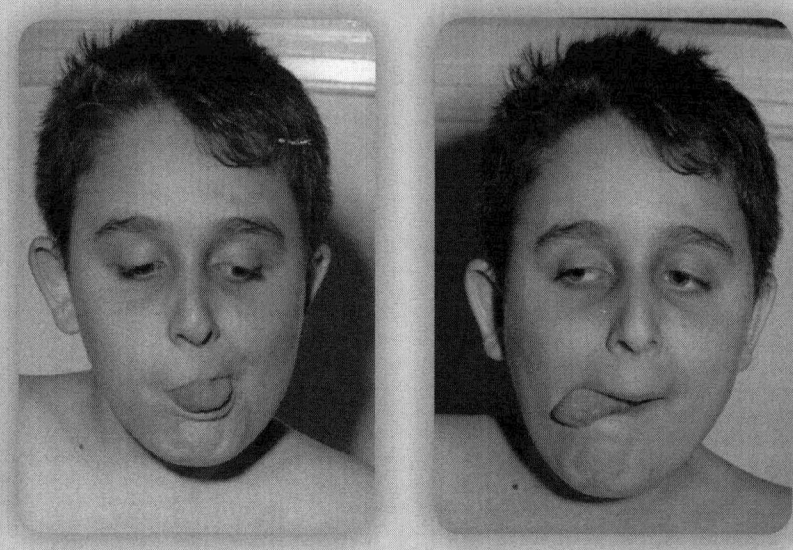

Feldenkrais exercises

Strength, importance and dedication

At first I was impressed by the sheer strength, sense of importance and dedication I experienced in regard to the way John related to the many Feldenkrais classes he received. He was usually in the habit of going off to be alone or sit quietly for several hours after a class. When Mia or Shlomo or Gabi (the assistant) arrived, we had to leave. This wasn't easy for someone who had just been lying for hours on the rug in Yonatan's snug room, surrounded by art books and paintings, miniature soldiers and music. In Yonatan's room, I felt as if I were inside a womb: warm and safe. When I escorted Yonatan to Dr. Feldenkrais's office, I used to huddle in a corner of the waiting room on Nachmani St. in the hopes that Feldenkrais, with his eagle eyes, wouldn't notice me. I felt great fear and anxiety from any interaction with the method's founder.

Lior Pessach

In like manner my handicapped bones, muscles and joints need an environment which would allow them to be transformed into a new potential. My handicap needs a "refrigerator", a "stove" and, even more, a complete "kitchen" for it to become the kind of organism I desire.

I likened the bed to which I was confined to a "refrigerator". My bed served as an environment which, for almost twenty-four hours a day, maintained my disabled muscles, inert bones and paralyzed joints – all the ingredients for my "cooking" process. I likened my wheelchair to an environment which held my body for the specific purpose of transforming my disability – my wheelchair became the "stove". As for the "kitchen" in the metaphor, I used a natural setting – a park with trees, greenery, flowers, a river and a blue sky. This natural setting served as "kitchen" since it held both the "ingredients" (myself) and the "stove" (my wheelchair) as my disability was being converted ("baked") into a new potential.

It struck me that being disabled meant that what was paralyzed in me were human bones and human muscles. I reminded myself that human bones and muscles are of a nature which can produce from within itself almost any thinkable or even unthinkable mode of performance. The past record of the human body seemed remarkable in its versatility. Throughout history people have found a way to move as quickly as a horse through becoming charioteers, they have flown higher and quicker than any bird through piloting a supersonic aircraft, they have competed successfully with almost any fish through scuba diving and they have produced an incomparable grace of movement in both classical and modern ballet.

At Jonathan's Bar-Mitzva, 1964:
Arie Munitz, Elisabeth (Anna's sister), Allon Lev (cousin),
Anna and Jonathan

Allon and Jonathan

Next came the following distinction: On the one hand, nature displays an abundance of forms of life – daffodils, giraffes, butterflies, chimpanzees, irises, zebras, cacti, etc. On the other hand, there is another category of living entities – charioteers, scuba-divers, astronauts, horse-riders, pilots, taxi drivers, etc. Not one item from the above list was produced by nature, although many of them have shaped the world. All of these forms of existence were made possible only through man's capacity to invent. No one has seen a pilot emerge from nature as a daffodil does. Rather, pilots were produced after aircraft were invented, since without an airplane there would be no pilot. Only when man's creativity put together a chariot – that is, discovered a new potential in horses – did charioteers come into being. In short, I reflected on the human faculty which produces hitherto unknown potentials for life. Without this faculty, man would never have reached the moon.

I re-examined my two lists – I compared the list of natural forms of life with the list of humanly manufactured activities – such a comparison made it obvious that the humanly manufactured activities had many advantages over the natural ones. A supersonic aircraft could fly at swifter speeds and for greater distances than any robin, butterfly or mosquito. Very few giraffes or zebras could catch up to a racing car. An astronaut can get to places in the universe which are way beyond the range of any other living creatures on the face of the earth. It struck me that a supersonic aircraft could not only surpass the flying limits of robins and hawks, but was actually breaking the whole of nature's record in height and range of flight. Similarly, a

The downstairs neighbour

On the second floor of the apartment building on Bnei Moshe St. my father bought apartment no. 5; Bruria and Yaacov bought apartment no. 6. The entire apartment house was surrounded by sand, sand, and more sand.

There was no path and no street. There was Gamusin and Sheich Muniss and Givat Hakalaniot, and all very dangerous. At the end of Bnei Moshe St. was Municipal High School 4.

I could hear the bell ring before the beginning of the first class from home, then I would get up and run to school, always finding a place to sit near the door, because I was always late. One evening there was a knock on the door, and there stood a respectable-looking, elegant woman, outside the door.

'I'm sorry, I'm the downstairs neighbour, my name is Annie, and I'm Yonatan's mother. I was wondering if you would mind if Yonatan registers for the same class as you. If you don't mind, we'll register him, and then when he's sick and can't come to school, you'll be able to help him make up the work.'

And that's exactly what happened.

Noga Meyerovitch-Cohen

racing car could break speed records not only for mankind but for the whole of the animal kingdom. The record in covering large distances set by an astronaut would be a landmark in the history of the entire planet.

I continued to examine this notion of the human potential for manufacturing artificial "end products" from natural "raw materials". Then a strange implication of the general human tendency came to mind. Rather than directing our intention to remold nature solely in our environment, as in all the thoughts I had until then, we can also redirect this very same intention back upon ourselves – upon our very own nature.

It occurred to me that I could define this human potential in physical terms – I could describe it as a biological concept.

I thought of the way in which modern man uses sight. Through our very eyes, we probe the universe billions of light years away. Our visual faculty is capable of covering such magnitudes through applying telescopes. Our eyes can choose to observe the world of the micro instead of the macro through applying microscopes rather than telescopes. We have enabled our seeing capacity to be present in "real time", when viewing live broadcasts on television coming to us from the other side of the globe (I imagined myself viewing live Olympic games taking place in China).

I considered the human capacity to see without all of this technology (without telescopes, microscopes, television cameras, computers or even movie theatres). Obviously, in the not very distant past, human sight was "naked" – stripped of all the equipment that nowadays allows it to cover broader scales and dimensions. In other words, in the

Noga, Jonathan and Lior

Yonatan came from a school for the disabled and the society of other crippled children. He wanted to integrate into regular society, but was afraid. From the very beginning we developed a personal relationship as well as a friendship among the circle of friends that grew up around him. These connections helped and supported the needs of us all.

Lior Pessach

past, the human eye could see as far as the end of the street rather than as far as the end of the universe. We could see only our immediate neighbors rather than the whole of Napoleon's army, as seen in the movies. At this point the critical question arose: What was the process that took a limited biological faculty such as sight, and transformed it into the extraordinary visual world in which we live today? What was it in us that could revolutionize human visibility in such a dramatic way?

As I pondered this question, I noticed that, as human beings, we can regard our biological make-up as "raw material". I then observed a general rule typical of mankind's way of relating to this "raw material". We intend to transform the "raw material" of our constitution into new ways of acting in the world. The kind of life we lead really depends upon what we intended to make of ourselves as "end-products". Our resulting broadened faculties have very little in common with the limited scope of the "natural" capacities out of which they grew. I considered the contrast between the limits of the moving capacity that anyone is naturally endowed with and its outcome once this capacity has been trained. Some people have trained their moving capacity to a degree whereby they can become acrobats or masters of the martial arts. Thinking can undergo a similar process. I considered the thought an infant might have: "I'm cold". "I'm hungry". "Where is my mother?" I compared these thoughts with the thinking capacity of an astrophysicist who grew out of such an infant. The thinking of the astrophysicist has been transformed into a faculty that can mathematically analyze the distinction between 1.22 and 1.23 of the first second of the existence of the universe.

Meeting a disabled child

I met Yonatan during the first days of school. We sat together in class – he next to the door in his wheelchair, and me on the other side of the room, next to my good friend Uri. At the break a large man with white hair came and carried Yonatan down the stairs in his wheelchair. When we offered our help, he agreed and he let us carry Yonatan's schoolbag. Arie, Annie's husband, carried him down alone, and the next day carried him up again alone. Only after a few days he gave in to our insistent pleading and allowed us to help him out a little.

Don't pick up [the chair], he said, hold it together with me.

That was my first close-up encounter with a disabled child, and my first lesson in the Feldenkrais method. In my own way I wanted to help more, but I settled for the little they asked of me. In this way, an opening was created – the possibility to help and develop a new kind of relationship.

High school, lots of kids, was a frightening and difficult place. For me my connection with Yonatan was a sort of need or necessity – an attempt to find some humanity within the threatening jail in which I found myself. At the time I didn't understand any of this. I only felt that it was the right thing to do. From there my life path developed and became interwoven with that of John, sometimes close sometimes from afar, but in a different direction from anything I could have imagined. For me, a 14-year-old boy, my connection with Yonatan within days went from helping a disabled boy to a deep meeting between the worlds of two teenagers: I was thirsty for intimate friendship and wanted answers to questions about self-identity. I also had a strong desire to penetrate the depths of the soul, which I experienced as a private riddle, which no one understood, including myself.

Lior Pessach

CHAPTER 2

DISABILITY

In this chapter I would like to try and show that an investigation into disability can cast new light into some dark corners of human nature in general. I believe that humanity is suffering at present from a certain "blindness" as to the nature of stillness. I would argue that understanding paralysis may provide a "torch" that everyone (that is, non-disabled people, included) can use in order to brighten these somber areas. At this point, I would like to give a few examples of "blind spots" that most, if not all, people suffer from. My claim will be that a remedy to such blindness can be found in following a new path which can lead us through the narrow corridor of paralysis into a broader destination – the world of stillness.

The first "blind spot" that I would like to try and explore has to do with the unchanging nature of faces. One can recognize a face after many years. One would instantly recognize one's mother even if one were separated from

Haim Mendelson, Lior, Haim Yechimovitz, Noga, Yoram,
Gadi and Jonathan near the Yarkon River

Jonathan and Friends: Yoram, Noga, Lior, Gadi, Haim

her for a very long time. That face might have become wrinkled, the hair might have whitened, and the expression may have lost some of its early cheerfulness. Despite all of these many changes, there exists an unmistakable aspect through which the face will be recognized as belonging to one's mother. This aspect will prevail even if the expression is shifting from one moment to another, if, say, an expression of sadness would turn into an expression of joy. Behind all possible expressions lies an unchanging presence which we would identify as the person we know. This aspect, which allows the face to be recognizable, obviously dominates all of the changes that can take place.

The unchanging aspect of a face is, obviously, its structure – the distance between the eyes, the proportion of nose to mouth, the shape of the forehead, etc. Yet, there is something misleading about the terms "structure", "distance", "proportion", "shape". All these terms seem to indicate abstract properties which exist only as ideas of the mind. However, one can physically see, hear and even hold the other person. There is something tangible in the act of recognition. It is the discovery or re-discovery of someone else who physically exists in the world. What one discovers or re-discovers, I would claim, is a structure, a distance, a proportion, a shape – all engraved in matter. These traits are identifiable only inasmuch as they are molded in bone. To be more specific, a face becomes familiar due to its being carved in a concrete skull.

I would like to explain why the issue of recognizing faces was raised in this context – an investigation into disability. I believe that we can have a better perspective of what is involved in understanding paralysis, if we

Carrying up the wheelchair

I met Yonatan on the first day of school, Grade 9 (Municipal High School No. 4, 1970-1974). A disabled boy arrived in a wheelchair, pushed by his father, who was trying to carry him up the stairs. This was his step-father, Arie. We – a group of students – Chaim Mendelsohn, Gadi Ravnitzki, Lior Pessach, Chaim Yechimovich and me – came to lend a hand. This one-time help turned into a permanent job -carrying Yonatan up and down the stairs to and from the classroom. From that day onward, for four years, every morning we carried Yonatan up the stairs and at the end of the school day, we carried him back down.

One day we decided that one of us would go to his parents and tell them that we would carry Yonatan up and down the stairs every day – and relieve Arie of this task. And in this manner, a sort of cooperation formed between us. Arie or his mother would bring Yonatan to the entrance of the school and we would carry him up to the classroom in his wheelchair. This was the beginning of a friendship that grew and developed. We started to meet every Friday evening to play magnetic football. And that's how our talks started as well. We started having philosophical discussions. Someone raised the idea that the day would come when we would talk about income tax, and that would be a sign that life was truly over. Our group of friends, which formed around Yonatan, still exists today.

We very quickly found more ways to help. We wanted to give more and more. We were already connected to him, and our help became a matter of course. We helped him get to the movie theatre, and to his treatments with Dr. Moshe Feldenkrais. Yonatan was a friend like any other, and we often met together as a group.

Uri Nissel

realize the full meaning of the skull as a central issue in recognizing another person. The skull is obviously almost completely motionless. In this it resembles a paralyzed body. However, the skull is not only motionless, but this unmoving condition is also a significant part of a living process. Without a skull, the person would probably be dead, and yet, having a skull means being at least partially inert. Thus, without the inertia of the skull, there would be no life. In this, the presence of the skull in the life of any person reminds me of my condition. My body is very much inert and yet completely alive. My system is alive and as inert as is the normal condition of any person's head. The example of recognizing another person's face shows how the inert aspect of life can become useful. The capacity of relating to another person depends on the inertia contained in that person's face. This inertia is not a restriction on life, nor does anyone want to overlook it. Quite the opposite. When one encounters another person, one seeks (rather than overlooks) the other person's face, with all of its unchanging dimensions (proportion, structure and shape). In my life as a disabled person, I relate to inertia in a similar way – i.e. wanting to encounter it rather than overlook it – and yet the inertia I can encounter is far broader than that which is present in a face. My inertia permeates throughout my entire system and thus I am attempting to make this inertia proportionally more useful than the mere inertia of my skull. In my life, I am trying to increase the degree to which inertia can become instrumental, i.e. both in the way inertia is serving me and in the way I hope it can serve someone else. In this sense exploring disability is an attempt to increase by far the use which everyone

Meeting on Friday nights

In Grade 10, we were all together in one class. That's when all of our meetings began. On Friday evenings, after dinner, kids our age used to go out and party at discos, but in our group it was clear that we would all pile into Yonatan's room to sit and talk and argue about all kinds of subjects. And so the group was formed. Even after we finished school and each one went his own way, Yonatan was still the centre. We kept on visiting him, some more, some less.

Noga Meyerovitch-Cohen

Haim Mendelson, Yoram Guy, Gadi Ravnitzky,
Lior Pessach and Jonathan

else is in the habit of making of the presence of the face. Most people cherish the presence of faces in their lives – both the faces of others, or the face reflected in the mirror. I believe that the meaning of the face can be increased tenfold, through a more thorough realization of the nature of stillness.

Since all of us are constantly surrounded by the unchanging nature of familiar faces – the question could arise regarding what it is about faces that remains to be discovered. We all take for granted that a face will never be more than a face. We therefore need to realize what it is that can allow the constant meaning of a face to be dramatically increased. What is it about the stillness of faces we tend to overlook? Where in our view of things, is the blind spot that we have been ignoring? I believe that in the "still as a skull" presence of a face (through which we recognize people) there does exist an aspect we are unfamiliar with. This aspect is missing in the awareness of most, if not all, people. My claim is that the "skull stillness" of a face has, in truth, two aspects. We seem to acknowledge only one of these two aspects whilst ignoring the very existence of the other. We only possess an external image of the "skull stillness" when viewing them. The "skull" aspect we acknowledge is the unchanging nature of the faces of other people. In fact, we not only acknowledge this aspect, but we seem to continually make use of it, as we recognize neighbors, old friends, family members, etc. The aspect of faces we tend to use is the stillness of faces we encounter outside ourselves. There exists, however, an additional aspect which, I claim, we hardly ever pay any attention to. This aspect is our own

Noga, Yoram, Jonathan, Lior, Haim Yechimovitz
Haim Mendelson, Lior

Outings and friendship

During our high school years, we used to go on a lot of outings and hike all around the country. We deliberated about whether or not to tell John about these trips because we thought the fact that he couldn't participate might make him sad. John was smart enough to feel this. He brought up the subject himself, and let us know that everything was shared – even those experiences that he couldn't actually participate in with his physical body. In this way, the barrier was broken and ever since, we shared all of our experiences with John fully. We could talk, ask advice and discuss every subject, even personal ones; we even talked about our friendship.

Gadi Ravnitzki

face, or to be more precise, the unchanging ("skull like") nature of our own features. We do not possess a picture of ourselves from the inside, unless we trick ourselves by using a mirror which reflects us from the outside. We are incapable, for the most part, of recognizing ourselves as other people do, when they do, indeed, recognize us. It strikes me that through viewing faces we can see the identity of everyone but ourselves. How come the inner stillness of our own skull fails to convey to us an image which would make us recognizable to ourselves?

I believe that relating to our own face can reveal to us two radically different aspects of our selves. When we turn our attention to our own face we can witness a gap existing between an aspect we continually use and another aspect, which we equally possess, but do not know how to use. We seem to master in a considerable way the changes we can introduce into our own facial expressions. We experience our own freedom to smile, frown, blink or even put on a serious countenance. We have under our control not only the capacity to produce these expressions, but also the capacity of causing any one of these expressions to be transformed into another. Even as children, we take for granted how a smile can become a frown and then instantly return to the previous happy expression. From childhood on we seem to know almost everything about the changes that our face can undergo. As opposed to our total involvement in this changing aspect of our face, we do not seem to invest ourselves at all in the other aspect of our face – its unmoving side. Although we know how to thoroughly use our facial muscles, we seem to fail in

Besides being a close friend and good listener, with incredible analytical capabilities and a deep interest in almost every field, Yonatan was "a phenomenon". Despite his almost complete paralysis, he managed to reach heights of intellectual thinking and dive down to experience the most nuanced depths of human compassion. In spite of his physical limitations, in his mind, Yonatan mapped out an infinite number of details, data and facts, penetrating the heart of everyone he knew.

As someone who only very rarely left his room, he created his own world, through his sharp intelligence and fine diagnostic capabilities. You could talk to him about any subject: philosophy, art, music, literature and science. In Yonatan's expansive mind and heart, there was no intellectual or emotional area which he failed to conquer. Thus, he changed the perspective of almost everyone he spoke with, especially as regards everything related to "disability". Yonatan wasn't able to move, but no one knew more about movement than he did. By observing a person's voice, fields of interest, body language and facial expressions, Yonatan could draw – with great precision and sensitivity – a character profile of the person he was speaking with.

All of these things and more turned his small room in old north Tel Aviv into a place of pilgrimage for friends, acquaintances, artists, people from the sciences and the humanities, as well as therapists of the Feldenkrais method.

Eran Blacher

making any use of the bone that is equally present in us – our skull. Our skull plays a significant role, which we tend to ignore, in everything that we do facially. We do not profit in any way from the fact that behind all our changing muscular expression, there lies an unchanging bony layer that we equally possess. As a result of this shortcoming of ours, we regard the changes in expression of a face, brought about by its muscular movements, as being the symbol of life itself. We will remember a deceased person that was dear to us through that person's smile. However we will regard the skull of that very same face not as symbolizing that person's death. (At the very most, such a skull would be regarded by us as the appropriate symbol of a pirate's flag.) In other words, we tend to associate the bone-still nature of a skull only with death. A pirate's flag can demonstrate that we have not discovered the way in which stillness and life can be associated. I believe that living through a paralyzed system, as I myself do, could allow a better perspective of the way in which an absence of movement can vitalize rather than kill. My hope is that we have, within our potential, the capacity to reevaluate that which is depicted on a pirate's flag. We can reveal in our own self the life-giving dimension of the skull present inside our head.

The paralyzed condition of my body has allowed me, I believe, to have more access to the still presence of my own skull. I think that what has assisted me is the fact that most of my system is almost as still as my skull. Being disabled the way I am, I experience my limbs, torso, chest etc. as possessing a quietude which people hardly ever

Broadening horizons

Our group of friends from high school went on to the army, then to their academic studies. We met often with Yonatan. I wasn't involved in his heavy cultural subjects – music and philosophy – but just the mere contact I had with him pushed me to broaden my horizons. Among other things, I started looking at art books.

Uri Nissel

Discussion groups

Many of our mutual friends from school participated in our discussion groups during the 70s. We talked about disability, awareness, art, perception, music, man, the physical body and love. In one of our meetings, professors from the university participated: Menachem Brinker, Shlomo Biderman, David Baum, and Yakir Aharonov.

Sara Blacher

encounter. Almost all of my joints, muscles and bones are so completely immobile that they afford me the opportunity of experiencing a quietude of an unusual intensity. It is a tranquility that people would usually find only in the domain of their own skull. It is as if my skull had grown to the dimensions of my entire physical existence. In short, the stillness of my system is such that it presents itself to me as a "body-sized" skull. Consequently, the stillness permeating my skull is not to me a minute part of myself, which I can easily ignore. Instead, my "skull-stillness" has become a major aspect of my make-up which I cannot overlook.

The sense of a "body-sized" skull present in my entire system allows for a new proportion between movement and stillness. Such an abundance of non-movement introduces into my system a far larger portion of stillness than is usually the case. This uncommon form of existence revolutionized for me the very definition of stillness. It offers me an unconventional way of evaluating the nature of stillness. I believe that stillness is often perceived as sheer absence of movement. This attitude towards stillness is apparent in the way a parked car, a docked ship or an aircraft that has landed would be regarded by an onlooker. The stillness (i.e. the stationary condition of these vehicles) is evaluated (by such an onlooker) as an absence of the movement for which they were originally designated. An aircraft is an aircraft only in as much as it can fly, and the same can be said of a speeding car or a sailing ship. Very often I myself experience a similar attitude towards my life coming from people who encounter my condition for the

How much longer will I live?

And then Moshe [Feldenkrais] slowly stopped coming and I would come to Yonatan by myself. I used to talk to Annie a lot. I said to her: Tell me, do you think he knows what a difficult disease he has?

Because he never talked about it. She said: I don't think he knows. And then one day, while I was working with him, in the middle of the class, he said: So tell me, how much longer do you think I'll live?

I was a bit shocked and surprised, and after this happened I called Moshe and told him: Listen, next time you have to come with me. He said he would, and next time we went together. Then he said: I want you to stay in the room and see how I speak with him. While he was working with him, he suddenly came out with:

You don't know how much I envy you.

And Yonatan said: What? What is there to envy?

Moshe said: There are so many things that I want to do in my life and I don't know if I'll manage to do them during my lifetime, but you – whatever you want to do, you'll do much more than I'll ever manage to.

Then Yonatan said: I don't understand.

And Moshe answered: Look, I want to write a book, but I don't have the time. I want to study music, singing, swimming, painting and so many other things, and it's just not possible. And why? Because of phone calls, income tax, all kinds of problems; people come and disturb me, and you – all of your time is in your own hands and you can do whatever you want. The world comes to you, so you don't have to go so far to reach everything.

first time. They regard me as a parked car. I believe they feel that a car that cannot move has very little value. Likewise, they consider that to possess a human body that cannot produce its own movement is a way of existing that is quite meaningless. In short, they feel that disability is an absence of a dimension that is essential to the very nature of life. They do not regard me as a mere parked car, but rather as a "broken down" car – a car that is "irreparable". My condition, viewed from this perspective, is an irrevocable absence of movement. When I turn to my "body sized" skull, it opens up a radically different perspective. My system, when experienced personally by me (rather than being witnessed from the outside by an on-looker) turns the logic of this evaluation upside-down. It introduces a possibility of evaluating the movement present in walking, climbing stairs and even in playing football – as a mere absence of stillness. I am sure that to a person who takes bodily movement for granted the statement "an absence of stillness", when referring to that person's movement, would appear, at least at first, both artificial and ridiculous. I would remind such a person of a certain situation which is very common (i.e. almost everyone experiences it). What I have in mind is a day spent in a secluded place, such as a forest or any other very quiet location in the country. At the end of such a day, as one travelled back to the bustle of the city, there would be a moment of transition from one environment to another. As one approached the first traffic jammed highway, on the way back to town, one would have a sense that something that was present earlier on is now being taken away. It was as if the stillness that was present in the "secluded country-side" situation was

There was one other time when I phoned Moshe and said to him: You need to come because Yonatan is asking…this was when one of the friends, Shabtai, was killed in the war. Yonatan was traumatized and couldn't cope with it. Moshe came and helped him.

Mia Segal

Moshe Feldenkrais and Mia Segal

suddenly shattered by the noise and movement of the motorway. In short, one can feel the "absence of stillness". This quite ordinary situation bears some resemblance to the experience that I undergo through paralysis.

My paralysis allows for a very large arena, in which very little movement can be found. Thus, I have a sense of my paralyzed system as a contest in which stillness prevails to a degree rarely found elsewhere in human life. I believe that when looked at from my inert point of view, stillness discloses some of its secrets, that can hardly be noticeable from a different vantage point. This blown up image of inertia, which I hold as a disabled person, affords me a closer appreciation of what stillness truly consists of. I experience stillness as a real substance that exists materially. I feel it as a "hard fact". I sense stillness as a force whose impact causes certain transformations to take place in the world. The impression I have of my own immobility is of an organ which accumulates great quantities of stillness. What occurs before my very eyes is that once stillness is amassed it acquires a more obvious capacity to effect the physical world. I witness the presence of stillness permeating my motionless members. Accordingly all around me an absence of stillness becomes very apparent. Thus, what I undergo when feeling the inertia of my own body presents to me the movement which activates my environment, as a "scarcity of stillness". The movement outside me takes on an expression of a "vacuum", emptied of any outcome of stillness.

What does he know about ballet?

Yonatan had a special relationship with my children. He could speak with my daughter about music and ballet. What did he know about ballet? He knew. He just knew.

And about painting and those kinds of things. With my son, he used to speak about basketball, as if he himself were a basketball player. It was really amazing. And the children – when they were talking to him, they would forget they were talking with a child who had never done any of those things. It was simply wonderful, moving, like magic. He hypnotized them.

Mia Segal

I experience my paralysis as an organ inherently sensitive to the characteristics of stillness. Being almost constantly bedridden, my paralyzed foot develops a profound intimacy with the stillness of the surface on which my body is placed. Through its contact with the mattress, my paralyzed foot, being equally inert, shares some hidden secrets that are held in the mattress. When explored in this way by my paralyzed foot, the inertia of my bed reveals to me its own stillness as existing – as a true reality. Stillness, when investigated by a paralyzed organ, proves to be a tangible presence – a substance that can be measured and even weighed. My paralyzed foot, through applying its own quality of quietude, seems to detect within the bed an ever-growing quantity of stillness. My disability has at its disposal a means of assessing the precise amount of stillness present at any given moment in my bed. Any increase in the quantity of stillness is measured by my foot through discerning an augmented impact that the bed has upon me. I sense my life undergoing a more radical transformation, whenever more stillness is absorbed by my foot.

I regard my investigation into disability as a quest, looking into an aspect of life that all people share. I regard this quest as magnifying something essential that exists in everyone. In every person's constitution there is a whole side which is still by its very nature. The make-up of every person includes bones, whose nature is still. Our bones move only in the joints, but maintain the stillness of their

Entrance exam

In 1994, I came to work with him. First of all, he gave me his entrance exam, and talked with me about Witgenstein and Spinoza. When I started working with him, I told him: Listen, with these kinds of entrance exams, no one will come. It was a very, very high standard. I somehow managed to integrate into the group of very impressive people who were there.

Benny Chor

Hunger for information

As the years advanced our game playing decreased and our talks deepened. Jonathan had a raging hunger for information about History, biographies of various celebrities, geography, politics, enrichment of vocabulary (in both Hebrew and French), the everyday lives of people, either close to him or not, and many other fields.

I failed to understand that Jonathan was the source of normality in relationship, in behavior. Everything was normal: the interest he showed in other people and in their difficulties was normal, his acute sense of humor was normal, his sharp repartee on every subject was normal.

When he started his studies at Ironi Dalet high school, all of a sudden his life was enlarged, thanks to the magnificent group who spontaneously surrounded him, and continued supporting him for the rest of his life. He enlarged his own life constantly, thanks to his personal charm, and always under the secrecy constructed in his childhood.

Allon Lev

shape and structure. This stillness will endure, not only throughout the whole of that person's life, but far beyond it. Paleontologists can discover skeletons whose intrinsic stillness has maintained itself over a period of millions of years. These skeletons have hardly changed at all over this almost unlimited time span. Each one of us carries within himself such a skeleton – each person throughout his entire life witnesses only a small fraction of this unchanging way of existing. Everything that one can witness of the stillness of one's skeleton is a mere tip of the iceberg. At the very most one would witness 100 years of the existence of one's skeleton. However, the time dimension in which this very same skeleton will maintain its stillness is far broader than anyone can imagine.

The stillness of one's skeleton might endure for several million years. Thus, when one observes one's skeleton, one is looking into a small fraction of a still presence of tremendous endurance. In truth, one is facing a vast stillness even if one fails to appreciate it. A great part of ourselves is still (skeleton, facial expression, skull, etc.). However this stillness is not experienced as having an impact on our lives – it doesn't play a significant role in what we do. Stillness hardly appears in the repertoire of things what we are trying to accomplish. In short, we ignore the intrinsic stillness of our make-up. The purpose of this investigation is to use disability as a means to unravel the nature of our intrinsic stillness.

Jonathan (left) playing ping pong couples with Lior Pessach (right)

The healthiest of men

I learned so much from him. Sometimes people come to me and say this hurts, that hurts, and then I tell them about the healthiest man I ever knew. I tell them about Yonatan. He was really the healthiest man I ever knew. He lived a full and complete life.

Mia Segal

CHAPTER 3

CONFINEMENT

My first significant experience of disability was that of an increasing confinement to my bed. Around the age of five I began to gradually lose my capacity to sit up and move about in my wheelchair. By the age of thirty I could hardly spend more than two to three hours a day not lying on my back. As these lines are being written I am not only confined to bed for almost all of the time, but all I can do is move my eyes and use my voice in speaking. My torso and limbs have by now become almost completely motionless.

At first I saw the course my malady was taking as leading only to destructive results. It seemed to me that my deteriorating condition would eventually render me incapable of enjoying most of what life had to offer. I was convinced that I would never again be able to contribute to any constructive human endeavor. In short, my feeling was that my physical condition was gradually robbing my life of almost all possible meaning.

Disability and Ideas

John wanted to spread his principles in the theoretical level. In the 1970s, when Israel had only one TV channel, he was invited to appear on Ehud Yaari's talk show. The plan was that each interviewee was photographed once and in one shot. After the recording Ehud Yaari was not pleased. In his opinion, John's disability had to be mentioned in order to explain. John objected. Ehud yaari asked for my help. I argued with John and explained to him that the best way to explain his ideas was to give an example from himself. John objected persisitently. It was the first and only time that the interview was recorded three or four times, and between each recording the same argument with John aroused. On the way back from Jerusalem John was furious with me. I'm not important, he said repeatedly, the ideas and philosophy matter.

Gadi Ravnitzki

I was telling myself that disability was equal to not being able to walk, either at home or in the street, not being able to dance or participate in sports, not being able to hold most jobs, not being able to raise a family, not being able to...etc etc. At a certain point I realized that this attitude to my growing paralysis was wrong, at least on one score. It occurred to me then that I could give myself the same list of incapacities (not being able to...) in describing other situations in life. I could imagine myself seated in an elegant concert-hall enjoying great music. I could be telling myself that for as long as the music lasted, I was not able to walk around either at home or in the street, nor was I able to dance or participate in sports. In order to do all the things I couldn't whilst in the hall I would have to give up the music and leave the concert. Another situation that I thought of was that of an Arctic explorer on an expedition for several years who consequently could not hold a 9 to 5 job or raise a family, unless he ceased exploring and returned to civilization. From these two radically different examples I concluded that not being able to walk, dance, participate in sports, hold a job and raise a family would be quite a poor account of what it is to listen to beautiful music or explore the world. In other words, one can't give an adequate description of any situation simply by stating what that situation is not. Similarly, it became obvious that I could not afford to give myself an account of my disability just by listing all those things that I could not do. I needed to describe what disability was rather than what is was not.

I realized that most of what I expected of life was relevant only to people with a normal physical constitution. Since such expectations were not relevant to my condition, I understood that I must develop new expectations that

Jonathan's drawing from school

might not be relevant to other people and yet would be appropriate for me. Ultimately, I designed a new purpose for my life. My new aim was to arrive at the most authentic representation possible of my disability.

The accumulation of distances

When one is present in stillness one feels that different distances are integrated in a new way. One might have arrived there coming from a great distance, and this far place where one came from takes on the existence of a place very nearby. There is a transformation of the distance into a sense of proximity – of being close by. It is not only with those points which are distant because one travelled from them in order to arrive where one is. There exists also the "making near" of points to which one is heading in order to attain them in the future. These distant future points seem to come near – they seem, as well, to exist in one's proximity. This "nearing" (as opposed to distancing) means a sense of an accumulation of all the time that was needed to arrive here and all the time that is required to reach a future destination. All of this time is accumulated (or condensed) within that small span that will normally require the covering of very short distances, distances that exist in one's immediate proximity. The time required to cover far distances is all brought together, gathered and fused within those narrow boundaries of movement, that normally encapsulate only a minimal covering of space (which usually takes a very short time). In a word, in a very short time one can hold time spans that would normally belong to prolonged processes that would take a long while when practiced outside of stillness.

Yontatan's film

I met Yonatan through a mutual friend, Judy, and it slowly became clear that I was meant to be the photographer and professional, in charge olf producing Yonatan's film. Our connection branched out to embrace other fields. Yonatan taught me about Spinoza and about spatial movement.

Many times, I showed him my work – paintings and film – and I received the criticism of a wise person. At this time, I was a film student in Tel Aviv and I didn't have a cent. We used to meet and discuss the film. Yonatan would utter picturesque philopophical ideas, while I would try to ground them in the real world. In exchange for the days when we shot the film, I extracted a small fee; this weighs heavily upon my conscience until today. We spent 6-7 days filming with H8 cassettes.

On location, everything took place according to the wishes of the main actor, who was also the producer. The script was engraved on Yonatan's memory. The production company included Shoshi, a driver, and other friends who came to help. We took moving longshots along the banks of the Yarkon, and strolled along the beach's sandy cliffs. We filmed at the Safari, next to the tiger's cage, shooting one important take over and over again, trying to get it right. Suddenly, the tiger urinated from behind, as tigers do. Both Yonatan and the camera got wet.

Yet, the heart of our connection was actually a fragile mobile which I made for him out of shells. Yonatan made sure it was hung within his field of vision. The warm drafts in the room moved the mobile in slow circles throughout the day for many years.

Mati Lahat

The Horizontal World vs. the Vertical World

The horizontal world (horizontal space and horizontal time) has the qualities of the physical domain – linear, like a street – houses follow each other arranged side by side, each one existing separately from one another. Consequently, things belonging to the horizontal world produce distance – both in space and in time. They are far away from each other, requiring a great deal of time to bridge this distance. The Experience: dissipation, both in time and in space, the scarcity of both.

The vertical world (vertical space + vertical time) has the qualities of the mental domain – circular, like a city center – cars, buildings, ideas, regulations, policemen, merchants, clerks, etc. – all merging into a single entity, all held together by gravitation – not dispersing throughout the universe, but staying together in a constant mesh – interactions between various elements producing fusion – things coexisting both spatially and temporally. Consequently, things existing in the vertical world produce closeness, both in space and in time. They exist near each other, requiring very little time to reach any destination. Wherever one goes in the vertical world, one actually stays in the same circle, continuously belonging to the same overall entity. The Experience: an abundance of time and a great accumulation of space.

★

Jonathan's drawings from school

I visit a natural resort which has a river that runs through it. The southern bank of the river (where I am situated) has a park which contains a good number of trees. The northern bank (which I view from a distance) is a very large meadow containing some sport facilities. On most days there is a lot of activity taking place in that meadow, with many people participating for most of the time. In this way a sharp contrast exists between the southern bank with its profound quietude and the northern bank with its ceaseless activity. As we approach the southern bank the movement of the wheelchair, and even more, the walking presence of my partner pushing it alone, produces in me a sense of a horizontal (or linear) space and time. Time passes gradually as we continue on our course, ticking away minute by minute in a monotonous way. The space of the small wood offers itself, accordingly, in a linear pattern with trees arranged side by side, one following the other. As the tranquility of the small wood becomes more dominant, and our movement gradually comes to a halt, I find myself entering a vertical space and vertical time. Perhaps the clearest way of describing verticality in both its aspects is to compare it with the horizontal world. Such a comparison is also apt, because at this stage a turning point is achieved – a shift from the horizontal to the vertical. When existing horizontally the river has two banks which are present, one north of the other, or the other south of the former – with the river separating the two and thus keeping the respective properties of each bank within its own bounds. However, when existing vertically the two banks tend to manifest some new aspects. Whereas horizontally the banks are related in a north-south pattern,

Yonatan – Director and main actor

Yonatan had a volunteer who drove him around, and I was the pilot of his wheelchair, mainly when we went on outings. Yonatan didn't allow everyone to wheel him in his wheelchair. He needed to feel he was in safe hands.

And this was my job when we made the movie. There was a scene that involved rock climbing. I built the rock from paper mache, according to the strict dimensions Yonatan gave me. The aim was to conceptualize the power of gravity in relation to a disabled person. Yonatan had very specific thoughts about this notion, which he tried to convey in the film. He wrote the script, he was the director, the actor; his stage directions were very specific and we were not allowed to deviate from them. The location and angle of the shot was taken into account. The hours we spent filming were wonderful, fascinating.

When Yonatan first saw the film, he wasn't satisfied. The idea had not been conveyed clearly enough, he felt; we needed to revise the script. In this way, we wrote down endless pages of ideas that received almost infinite development and attention.

Yonatan was a perfectionist and wanted the processing of the idea to be perfect. For this reason, the film was never finished. He wanted to go back and complete the work. His plans could have filled many years with activity.

Shosh Foyerlicht

this relationship when existing vertically seems to render itself as a more complex entity. The banks, when existing in the vertical world, are related in that the tumultuous northern bank seems to hold some of the quietude of the peaceful southern bank, and vice versa – the peaceful wood is related to the sport facilities in that it seems to have, as an inherent aspect of itself, some of the tumult that is produced by the sportive practices. Spatially, the vertical world reveals itself as accumulating the key aspects of the two spaces (the northern and the southern areas). Instead of these aspects being divided (as in the horizontal world) between the two banks – with the bustle belonging to the northern and the quietude to the southern – in the vertical world both peacefulness and commotion seem to fuse and co-exist on both banks. They seem to produce a new third aspect of the world (which I may coin peaceful commotion or bustling tranquility) which seems to prevail everywhere – both in the north and in the south. In this way the northern bank and the southern bank become one – the space in which they exist has neither a northern nor a southern direction to it (it is not linear in a north-south way) but instead offers a circular world where everything exists everywhere. In this sense the vertical world contributes a new way of relating – a relationship which instead of bridging a gap between separate spatial entities, fuses these entities so that they co-exist as a single spatial presence. The experience that such a fusion of spaces creates in me is of an astounding abundance of space – space does not seem to be "larger than life", but instead larger than itself, reaching beyond its own limits. The feeling is of overwhelming vastness of everything,

The Idea for the Film

In my ongoing dialog with Lior Pessach, my cousin and Feldenkrais instructor, we thought it was a good idea to make a film about the Feldenkrais method, so that people who were not familiar with the method could learn about it. Lior then told me about Yonatan, his childhood friend. I said I'd be happy to meet him – and maybe I'd be able to persuade him to participate in the film.

In this context, I came to meet Yonatan one hot and steamy summer's day in Tel Aviv. I entered through the yard and into his room and was immediately covered in sweat. In his room, there was neither a fan nor an air conditioner. I naturally began the small talk of a new acquaintanceship, but Yonatan cut to the chase right away, having no time, it seemed, for small talk. It took me a moment to understand where he was coming from. He asked me directly why I had come. I told him I was interested in the relation between the body and the soul and told him about my film idea. To my amazement, he told me he had already started a film project and had done thirti days of filming.

It was amazing. It was the kind of conversation you have only once or twice in your life; the things Yonatan said are still with me today. Yonatan was of the opinion that evolution had equipped us with a frontal lobe brain, that same part of the brain that allows us to learn and actually forces us to learn, and to continue learning, even during times of crisis, pain and despair. What do we do with all this knowledge and where does it go? To my great happiness, the knowledge and wisdom Yonatan accumulated during his lifetime isn't lost to the world, because Yonatan liked to write.

Shuka Glotman

growing beyond its own dimensions and thus reaching out to fill the entire world with its own unique presence. When a spatial "relationship" is produced vertically (i.e., a vertical relationship between spaces is brought about), a vertical fusion of spaces replaces the horizontal way of relating to spaces through the introduction of the mere bridging of gaps between spaces.

Time, as well as space, undergoes a transformation as I experience leaving the horizontal world and entering verticality. Here, again, there exists a clear turning point (between the horizontal and the vertical), and consequently it would, therefore, be once more only fitting to compare horizontal time with vertical time. At first my wheelchair is travelling along on the route which leads from my house to the park which awaits us on the southern bank. As we progress on our way, I feel both my partner and myself, as completely immersed in what I coin "Horizontal Time". "Horizontal Time" offers the past and the future as two distinct entities, differing in most respects and sharply separated from one another. The past, when identified with "Horizontal Time", is already known. In the case of our outing, "Horizontal Time" holds that set of already experienced sensations which we shared as we were leaving my house and those that came to us as we were exploring all of the route we covered later on. All the smells, the hues, shades, colors and shapes that we had already encountered on our way, signify our past. All of them were experienced a short while ago and, thereby, they cannot but belong to the past of "Horizontal Time". By contrast, the future, when existing "Horizontally" (as it does – for as long as we travel on), holds within its bounds all that is yet unknown.

Effects

When John wanted to produce a film, I was assigned the role of the special effects man. Until today, I will never understand where his knowledge for directing and filming came from – how it is that he knew how to explain to others, in words, how he wanted the film to look.

Gadi Ravnitzki

As we make our way to the garden that we intend to reach, both my partner and myself share a "Horizontal Future" that does not contain a trace of the past. The way the park will smell today and the kind of hues and shades of color it holds for us, are still enigmatic since we have not yet reached our destination (being, as far as we are from the southern bank of the river). Everything on our way that is already known belongs solely to the past, whilst everything awaiting us inside the garden for as long as it remains unknown, cannot but belong to the future.

This division between past and future gradually disappears as we enter the small wood and my wheelchair slowly comes to a halt. The quietude pervading the small wood eventually overcomes all traces of the world of horizontality. Instead, the stillness inherent in my disabled condition seems to fully express itself, affecting the very nature of time. Here too, just as in the case of space, time seems to change and take on "Vertical" aspects. "Vertical Time" manifests a different relationship between the past and the future. Somehow I can sense echoes of the past reverberating into the future. What is even stranger is that I feel the future flowing backward towards the past. The past seems to be strongly colored by tones emanating from the future. Past and future seem to flow simultaneously backwards and forwards, emerging as a single continuity which embraces all that is to be. Every single moment contains all the moments that have already passed and all those that are yet to come. Thus, each moment becomes larger than itself, broadening its scope as it encompasses all the moments of the past and all the moments of the future.

A model for independent existence

Jonathan consulted with me and other friends on the development model of independent existence. The model was based on close friends, volunteers, caregivers, a Philippine caregiver. Jonathan wanted to find his help by himself. He wanted to interview many caregivers so he will have a reserve to depend on. All his life he was looking for caregivers, he interviewed dozens of them, and occasionally would take one for a trial period. I was sent to hang posters all over Petach Tikva to spread his message. It took months to teach a caregiver how to deal with Jonathan and hold him correctly.

Uri Nissel

The Wheelchair

Two stories, each narrating a different tale about horizontality. One narrative unrolling between the person wheeling me and myself, a tale unfolding behind me. The second narrative unrolling in front of us – both of myself and of the person wheeling me. The person wheeling me and myself sharing two distinct journeys – the back journey occurring between us and the front journey occurring ahead of both of us. The "Back Journey" is a story which revolves around that person's treading the path and the resulting revolution of the wheels. The "Front Journey" encapsulated the turning wheels and the perspective which both of us have of the horizontal way we are about to cover. The two narratives are distinct in that the "Front Journey" does not involve the treading of my partner and the "Back Journey" excludes the vista of what is to come ahead of us. As they shift into the vertical these two journeys ("Back" and "Front") acquire autonomy – they no longer remain as the two halves of a single movement. Verticality is to me a state where each of the two narratives is orientated independently in relation to the seat of my wheelchair. When moving horizontally the seat of the wheelchair acts as what the two "Journeys" have in common – exists as a "common denominator" when both form together forward movement. The stillness of the very same seat – its inert distance from the ground is what introduces the breaking apart of the two. Vertically they no longer have for me the meaning of what is happening either "behind" or "in front" since vertically the terms "in front" and "behind" no longer hold. It is as if the "Back Journey" were a piece

Distribution of work

Yonatan distributed the work so that none of the friends and volunteers would feel overwhelmed. Relatively, the tasks assigned to each person were few, so as not to be a burden and so that people wouldn't try to get out of doing the work. This was one of the things that helped to preserve the system for 45 years.

Danny was paid as a caregiver. Yonatan asked Shoshi to take out an envelope and prepare Danny's payment, together with a receipt, which Danny needed to sign. Because Yonatan was meticulous, he asked Shosh to come a week before and practice giving Danny the envelope.

Uri Nissel

Jonathan's notes stand

of a jigsaw puzzle and the "Front Journey" a completely different piece of the same picture. Each of them is present separately like two pieces of a jigsaw puzzle that do not of necessity hold together. The two narratives are introduced by the gravitational pull into the world of verticality. In the world of verticality each of these "two Journeys" takes on a life of its own.

Actually, the entirety of my paralyzed condition is invested in what occurs within the bounds of the "Back Journey". I can sense through the wheelchair my partner wheeling me along and I feel her doing so just because I am disabled. In other words, her footsteps not only indicate her position behind me but, even more so, they signify what might be the most meaningful fact of the entire outing, my not being able to move myself by myself. Consequently the "Back Journey" becomes a context which draws to it everything in me that is paralyzed. Therefore, this context emphasizes that aspect of the wheelchair which is as inert as I am – its unchanging relationship to the gravitational field. As a result, verticality prevails in the "Back Journey", transforming my relationship with my partner from a moving (or horizontal) relationship to a non-moving (or vertical) encounter.

Side by side with my involvement in the "Back Journey" which revolved around the figure of my wheeling partner, I also relate to a context in which my partner is not physically positioned – the territory lying in front rather than behind my wheelchair. The "Back Journey" was relevant solely to my disability, leaving uninvolved the other aspect of my organism – the little movement I still have. What was irrelevant to the "Back Journey" is the fact that the

Jonathan's reading stand

wheelchair is being driven forward but just this fact, becomes central when considering the "Front Journey". The wheelchair is moving towards those new territories which the journey is aimed at. What my partner and I see simultaneously ahead of both of us can belong only to the "Front Journey" since what lies before us consists of yet untraveled territory waiting for us to move into it.

The Void that Transcends Space

As the outing begins, being wheeled by my companion gives me a strong impression of my paralyzed legs. Their paralysis expresses itself as a sensation of their being non-legs, non-legs with a sense of utter blankness to them, non-legs that cannot walk (as my companion's legs do). Their knees cannot fold and extend (as her knees do) and they cannot even envisage themselves as standing upright when stopping to walk (as she does every time she reaches a pedestrian crossing).

Everything I see around me, everyone who is not using a wheelchair but simply walking in the street, is using a pair of legs. This fact emphasizes the gap between legs and non-legs. When this outing begins my non-legs are a non-sensation, since they do not perform in any way, nor serve any purpose. They give me a sense of blankness, of there being nothing in the lower part of my body.

At the next stage, three-dimensional non-legs (i.e. non-legs that have a concrete place in space) that emerge out of the initial blankness (i.e. out of the initial non-sensation of my legs).

Everything his way

Yonatan wanted to know everything that was important to his survival, for example, he was interested in the rights of foreign workers. He studied and researched everything. He learned about the video player he bought, about the remote control that would be most suitable for operating the devices he used. When there were changes in the bus lines, he got the new information and learned all of the bus routes so that he could advise his new caregivers.

All of his correspondence with the authorities, he would write with Moshe Blacher. He made a point of indicating new paragraphs and punctuation, and everything was written in his own words. He wasn't willing to accept any other wording.

Shosh Foyerlicht

This emerging of three dimensional non-legs (out of their previous blankness) takes place when the walking ability of my companion becomes more relevant – when through her walking, she starts wheeling my wheelchair and myself. Just as walking is three-dimensional (it can happen only within the bounds of space), three-dimensional non-legs can come into their spatial being only within the context of walking (of being wheeled).

My non-legs or the sense of the two blank entities that comprise the lower part of my body, are diametrically opposed to not being able to walk, run or jump – what I call having non-legs – at first seems to impoverish my life. As I go deeper into the experience I find that having non-legs enriches my life in that it offers a domain special to disability. The domain that I related to through my non-legs is what I call "non-experience".

I will first depict the domain of "non-experience" in order to facilitate an understanding of what I mean by "non-legs".

I believe that each one of us – every person – accumulates many experiences for instance: running, walking, that we gain through a life-long encounter with reality. In this way, we form a large body of experience. The scope of our experience is, however, limited. It is kept within the bounds of the life we go through individually. We don't always think of it, but most people we encounter during the day at the bus stop or in a supermarket queue or just sitting down in a café have accumulated on that very same day a whole range of experiences that have very little to do with ours. They have loved other children, had arguments with other wives or husbands, have looked out on a different view from their own apartment windows, and so on.

Ina the Caregiver

Ina took care of Yonatan from 1997 until his last day. She was living with her family in Netivot. One day she saw an ad: "Wanted: Caregiver" in the Russian newspaper. In the first interview, Yonatan asked her if she was planning on moving to Tel Aviv, what her life plans were, and what she likes to do – and he immediately gave her the job. After ten years of work, he told her that he had given her the job because she told him that she liked Russian and French authors and art.

Every time she borrowed a book from the library, Yonatan would ask her what she thought of the book. Upon returning from a trip abroad, she would tell him everything she had experienced and seen. She was like his glasses, looking out upon the world. Ina says she got a lot of good energy from Yonatan. Although she sometimes got so angry that she wanted to leave, he always managed to persuade her that the anger didn't spoil their relationship. He learned to understand her moods, and helped her on the difficult days. He felt what she was feeling. When she was about to get divorced, he advised her about what to say to her lawyer, as if he had gone through the experience himself.

Ina got a lot of support from him. She underwent a 9-month training period; it was only after this period that Yonatan allowed her to touch him. During his final years, she was his main caregiver. This began when he was brought to the hospital and Gala, his main caregiver at the time, disappeared. Danny, another caregiver, Ina and Yonatan's mother went with him, and Ina accompanied him the entire time he was in the hospital. According to Ina:

He wasn't like anyone or anything else.

Yonatan would phone her at all hours and in every situation. He had all of her numbers -at her parent's house, her sister's house, in Moscow, in Tel Aviv. He always worried about her and took care of her, and knew her every mood.

I call blankness that non-experienced reality which each one of us is exiled from. Consequently, our life has, as a rule, a dual reality. It holds a body of experience and side by side with it a body of non-experience. Whereas one of the elements is all that we experience, the other element always present in our lives is non-experience. Each one of us carries a body of non-experiences reality as central to the individual life which each person lives. This body of non-experience never leaves any one of us. It keeps on following us always and everywhere as if it were our shadow.

Let us think of a child who is in the habit of walking daily up a hill in order to get to school, another child might need to walk downhill and a third child might walk along pavements that are remarkably level. Since each of the three children could follow only one of these three ways of getting to school, each would, when the year was over, end up with a different kind of experience of that "walking" is at the end of the year. In other words, each of the three meanings of walking is reached through the individual child's own experience. However, each child not only has an individual life and therefore an individual experience. Each child also misses the experience gained by the other children – they may all study in the same school, but nevertheless each inhabits a different world of personal experience. So that with any three children whose lives we might choose to observe, we will inevitably see that any two children, as the case may be, will be exiled from the third child's experience of walking. For each three children, two will hold the third child's experience of walking as their own "non-experience" – as an experience of walking

I could have been your father, he used to say to her.

They were connected like very close friends. Sometimes Yonatan would get angry; sometimes she would be angry. She would talk and he would listen. Afterwards, he would explain to her how complicated the whole situation was, and she would accept his opinion.

One of Ina's responsibilities was to file every piece of paper, all reproductions, cassettes and letters. Just to be on the safe side, Moshe Blacher would also file. Letters, formal papers and documentation – everything was photocopied several times and filed away in more than one place.

Shosh Foyerlicht

that they have never had and may never have throughout their entire lives. Therefore, with each experience (in one child) at least two portions of "non-experience" will be produced (in at least two other children). This example shows that "non-experience" grows far more prolifically than experience. As a result, the world must contain far more "non-experience" than "experience".

As long as my immobility is not in contact with movement, I experience a sense of utter blankness. The blankness of my motionless world is all-pervasive: In other words, it cannot have limits of any kind, since nothing can separate itself from such an experience of totality – the totality of blankness. As long as limits are not present, as long as there are no limits, I remain confined to the world of blankness. In order to break out of this confinement to blankness, my paralyzed system is in search of a point in its own world which would offer an opportunity to discover limits and open up to what is on the other side of such a border. The world of my paralysis is entirely held within the confines of my wheelchair. As my paralysis explores my wheelchair in order to break out of the totality of blankness, it discovers one aspect of the wheelchair which is not limited to the world of paralysis. This one aspect of the wheelchair is in direct contact with the three-dimensional world of movement – movement that occurs within a limited space. The three-dimensional existence of my non-legs comes into being only when I am under the influence of what is happening.

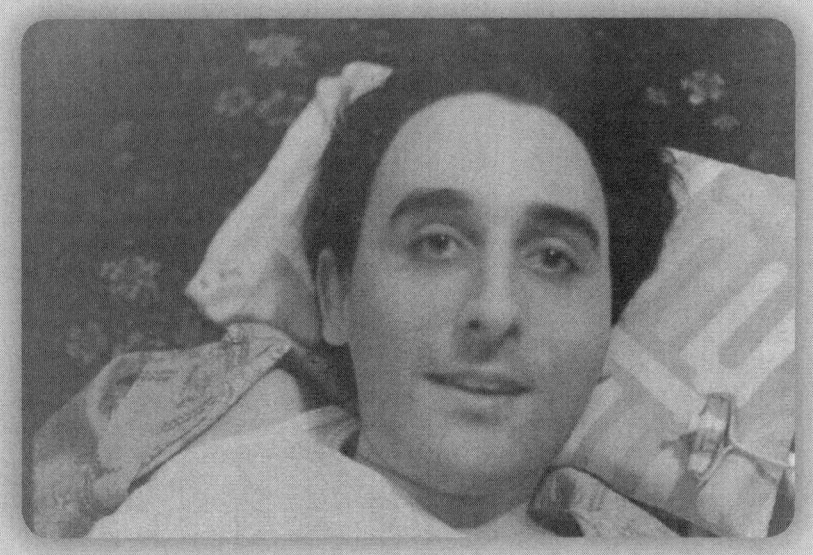

Jonathan

In addition to the examples of sleep and early memories, I would like to introduce a third example which will be more comprehensive. It will refer to life in its entirety, rather than referring to episodes in life – the span of sleep and the span of early memories.

The obvious fact about life is that it consists of a finite period of years. What is less obvious, however, is the fact that prior to life (before one's birth) and subsequent to life (after one's death) there exist two vast periods of time, both of which are outside the range of our personal experience. Much of what existed before life and much of what will exist after life have, nonetheless, an undeniable bearing upon what one chooses to do in the day to day reality of one's life. In other words: that which no longer exists and that which does not yet exist, are both very much alive in the here-and-now. For example, although one was not alive during the years when Socrates was conducting his philosophical discussions in the marketplace, nor was one alive during the period of the French Revolution, one must be aware that other people, long dead, were personally affected by these events. Strange as it may seem, one can choose to be affected today by these now far-in-the-past events. One can now adopt the Socratic method of argument or follow the ideals of freedom promulgated in 1789. In this sense, one can say that ancient Greece, on the one hand, and eighteenth century France, on the other, cast deep shadows on one's life today.

Danny Filipino caregiver, 2013

Danny (Danilo) was Arie's caregiver. After Arie was moved to a treatment center, Danny began to care for Yonatan, and continued doing so until Yonatan's death, sixteen-and-half years later. From taking care of Yonatan, Danny learned a great deal about the human body, the skeletal structure, and mainly just how fragile the human body can be. From Yonatan, Danny learned about the importance with which he related to his life and his difficult physical condition. He learned the meaning of patience. Yonatan never raised his voice; he would patiently explain to Danny how to take care of him. And Danny wasn't the only one he taught.

Yonatan trained all of his caregivers by himself. At Yonatan's request, Danny took care of Yonatan's physical needs and helped his mother with household matters outside of Yonatan's room. When there were people in Yonatan's room, he used to ask for privacy. On outings, Yonatan's friends cared for him, rather than Danny. When on an outing, Yonatan preferred Danny to stay home with his mother, so that she wouldn't be left alone.

CHAPTER 4

SLEEP

The stillness of paralysis has a double impact on my life – it affects both the way I experience where I am (my perception of space) and my evaluation of time (the impression I have of a sequence of events as it takes place). As stillness affects the reality of my life, I find myself in a world that has an unusual sense of intimacy to it. Thus, whenever stillness transforms the space I'm in, I sense an out-of-the-ordinary atmosphere of closeness with everything around me. I can compare such an intense contact with my environment, to a life-long attachment established between an elderly person and objects which that person had the habit of using. An ambience of profound meaning seems to tie together that person's whole life with the objects that were being constantly involved with this process. A violin, for instance, can manifest such a liaison if it were played on for, say, sixty years by an elderly violinist. My bond with the world as a disabled person is somewhat different, however, from the one I have been comparing it to. Unlike

Yonatan gave Danny and Ina similar responsibilities, so that he wouldn't be dependent on just one caregiver.

There was always a certain distance between him and Danny. Yonatan didn't want Danny to feel that he was too dependent on him. Yonatan stopped being mobile when he broke his leg, after which he was bedridden and could no longer go out. From this time on, his activities also diminished.

Danny was dedicated to Yonatan. When Anna's health began to fail, he also took care of her. He has continued to care for her with great dedication until today.

Taken from an interview with Ina

the atmosphere existing at the end of a long life, the world I live in seems to be fresh with each new occasion. The intricate contact that I have with stillness creates between myself and my environment the meaning of a connection only recently made. Rather than pointing to a rich intimacy established in the past, it seems to point to the future – to the richness of an intimacy that is yet to be attained. Stillness is also manifest in the way I can appreciate time. As far as time is concerned, stillness seems to act upon my life by placing me in a childhood-like world. The time in which the events occur seems to grow beyond its normal dimension. As in early childhood, each incident which my life goes through occupies a very long interval. Time seems to embrace events that take on an almost symbolic significance. Even from a grown-up's perspective, every event appears to grow beyond its habitual rhythm and fill a greater amount of time. As in childhood, the events take on an uncommon magnitude through growing into larger-than-life proportions.

I think that space, when felt by a non-disabled person, is a "container" which holds all movements and all objects. Space, when perceived from a "normal" point of view, is what holds everything, without affecting anything held by it. It is a "neutral" container, i.e. a container that does not interfere with the things it "contains". At any given point in space, one can turn right or turn left, move forward or backward, up or down – all these directions are equivalent. Space is neutral in the sense that it does not bear any special impact upon the things that are held within it. As a disabled person I experience space in a different way. Together with its usual "containing" capacity the space I experience gains

Radiance

If there's one trait that characterized Yonatan, it would be that of benevolence or good will – being awed and inspired by life. This sense of wonder was obvious is in his voice, manner of speaking and intonation. There was a sort of radiance about him that not many people have, even among the healthiest and most successful.

There was a special spark in his eye, the light of someone who sees beyond the concrete reality. And maybe this is what kept him alive for so many years. His mother, Annie, also had a sense of greatness about her, no less than Yonatan, the same radiance and sense of wonder.

Rachel Pomerchik

an additional sense of direction. The "direction" I would like to introduce into my account of space is an aspect know by everyone. However, it is not recognized by most people as belonging to the domain of space. The "direction" aspect that exists in my space experience is instead perceived by all as belonging to their sense of time. Time is "direction bound": it inevitably begins in the past, continues in the present and heads toward the future. This single direction which time follows is irreversible – it will always begin in the past and end in the future and never begin in the future and end in the past. The space I find myself in as a disabled person imposes a particular direction on the world. I feel that the space of disability has its own direction which it introduces to my everyday reality. All of the space I live in follows a vertical direction. It is structured in an up-down mode. Being disabled, I always experience space in the same way – as "vertical space" – and I thus regard my experience as unavoidable. Since this experience differs from the "neutral space" that most people encounter in their lives, I would like to compare my experience of space with a side of life that everyone is familiar with. I believe that for most people the world of a dream has very often the same sense to it as the space of disability.

Many people report dreams in which they are flying or falling through space. This kind of dream can appear in a variety of forms. In the dream, one can be falling into a deep abyss or struggling against drowning in a large body of water or floating through the air or soaring in the sky. In all of these instances, the space of the dream is dominated by a strong sense of the vertical. In the world of the dreamer, verticality is felt everywhere – it prevails in each

Joy, generosity and kindness

Some people are extraordinary human beings. When we get lucky enough to meet them and spend time with them, they bring us to transcend ourselves and show us that even though life is a constant struggle, even if it is a desperate struggle – it can be accompanied by joy, generosity and kindness. That was Jonathan. He used to say he remembered our first meeting when he was three and I was five years old. We were in touch ever since – until the day he passed away. Our meeting was not a random date – his mother and my father worked together even before we were born.

Michael (Misha) Fingerhut

and every detail of the dream. The issue of verticality does not arise in the reality of everyday life. Generally, it is not a matter which captures our interest or involves all of our physical resources. Dreaming, it seems, opens the door to a dimension formerly un-noted. It is as if the vertical aspect of the world were kept hidden until the dream enabled it to manifest itself. If one visited Venice, one could say that "Venice is as beautiful as a marvelous dream".

If one were to say that the sites of Venice were "a dream come true", one would mean that the views encountered on the trip were so beautiful, that they were beyond the expectations one would normally have of life. The beautiful dream, to which Venice could be likened, would most probably have an "elevating" or "uplifting" atmosphere to it. A town, whose beauty could only be dreamt of, would appear in the dream as having almost celestial qualities. Everything about it would be light (as opposed to the downward tendency of heaviness), bright (existing as close as possible to the sun) and its design would consist of many majestic towers (like those of the Taj Mahal). Thus, when reality is compared to a beautiful dream, it not only takes on a vertical appearance, but it tends to point up. For as long as such a beautiful dream is being dreamt, it brings to the open a possibility whose impact was concealed in the everyday reality of the dreamer. This everyday reality holds within itself many vertical manifestations, all of which have an upward inclination. Through the normal course of events everyone encounters trees, tall buildings, layers of clouds in the sky appearing one above the other, ballet dancers who leap with the heightening of the musical phrase, etc. All of these instances, rather than exposing the verticality of

Organizing the bones

Whenever a change of place occurred, for example, when they would take Yonatan out of the car and into his room, it took a long while afterwards to reorganize his bones, reposition his body. This reorganization of his bones was important in order to avoid asthma-related breathing problems. I understood that it was difficult for Yonatan to sit up, and I learned how to position him so that he could sit and breathe easily long enough so that he could watch a movie or listen to a concert.

One of our achievements was when we managed to persuade him and his parents to take a holiday with us in faraway Nahariya.

In time, he also agreed to go out with us along the uneven paths bordering the Yarkon. This turned out to be a meaningful experience for me – as the person pushing his wheelchair – and also for Yonatan, who taught me to notice unpleasant movements that regular people are unaware of. Every bump and stone in the path was a source of pain and fear for Yonatan – requiring the reorganization of his limbs into a comfortable sitting position in his wheelchair.

Lior Pessach

the world, seem however to frown their upright stature in the flatness of the mundane. In our normal perspective of things, the vertical is not allowed to single itself out and be present independently, but only to exist as belonging in the rest of reality. The potential of the vertical to be manifest as a world in itself – as a total reality- exists everywhere. However, in no place outside a dream, does the vertical exist as fulfilling its autonomous potential. Only inside a dream is this potential carried out to its fullest expression, as the vertical is allowed to dominate the entire scene.

When one goes to sleep, one would normally expect not only that in the sleeping phase the dreaming of dreams will be made possible, but also that one would wake up in the same bed as one went to sleep in. During sleep one is "bedridden" as I am, due to my disability. Sleep can be regarded as a form of "paralysis" that expresses health rather than malady. Being "bedridden" means that one is prevented from carrying out everyday "horizontal" activities: neither in sleep nor in a case such as mine can one walk down the street, get to the nearest bus stop and travel on the first bus that comes along to a given destination. In order to perform such "horizontal" everyday undertakings, one would need to wake up or recover from my malady and participate in the normal "horizontal" repertoire. Nevertheless, both my malady and a sleeping situation can rule out the need for "horizontal" performance because of its interfering with the independent existence of "verticality". In a dream (as in my physical condition) "verticality" is no longer a mere aspect of the "horizontal world". The "horizontal world" is ruled out and, therefore, the vertical is allowed to stand alone, occupying the entire arena. I believe that the special

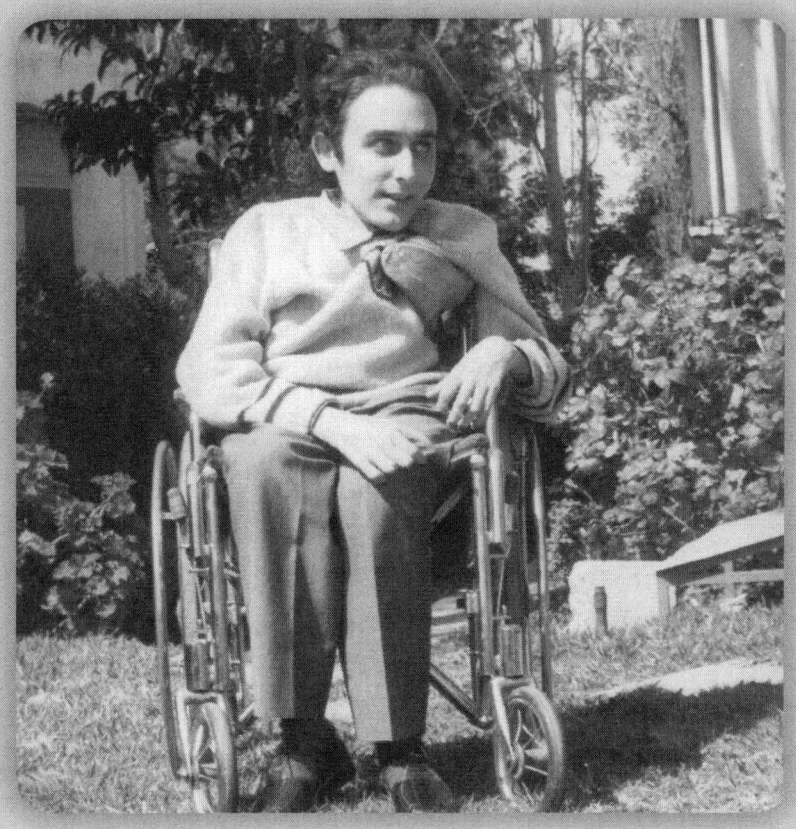

Jonathan, 1971

What's comfortable for him

They told us: Put his hand here; Yonatan will tell you what's comfortable and what isn't. He taught us.

Lior Pessach

textures revealed in the vertical glories of a beautiful dream may serve to demonstrate what such an independence can result in.

There is a fundamental gap, however, between the dream world and the world that I inhabit as a disabled person. The dream world exists only internally – once one wakes up and opens one's eyes, one sees a completely different world that exists outside. One then realizes that the dream, with all its special "dream-like" properties, exists only subjectively, i.e., it existed only inside the dreaming subject. One would ask, however, from where were these special properties derived? What was the source of the "dreamlike" quality of the dream? Are these qualities inherent only to the dream itself? I feel that my disability helps me in coping with these enigmatic issues. Disability provides me, from time to time, with short glimpses of the world outside, as possessing qualities similar to those of a dream. The world around me, when filtered through my paralysis, reveals a magical verticality which reminds me of the likeness, the brightness, and the tower-like configuration of a beautiful dream filtering itself through the brain. When the everyday reality pierces my system as a dream world would pierce one's mind during sleep, I have the sense that the source of dreams lies in certain aspects of the external world. These properties of the outside world are usually kept concealed and therefore are normally almost unnoticeable, but are nevertheless constantly present – out there in the world around us. Disability, I believe, can act as a "detector" which would avail these latent "dreamlike" aspects of the world, and allow them to become part of the repertoire accessible to a living human being.

Positioning the Limbs

Over the years, it wasn't always easy for me to understand what he wanted me to do regarding the positioning of his elbow, his arm and the rest of his limbs. It took time until I learned how to care for him correctly.

Ina the Caregiver

Organizing the Limbs

When we were at school with Yonatan, they taught us a little bit of Feldenkrais. I was with him in class, so I knew how to lift his leg, how to position his arm when he was sitting, so that he would be comfortable. They taught us how to hold his head and move it from side to side properly.

Noga Meyerovitch-Cohen

Let us consider a fact which most people would regard strange and yet to me, being a disabled person, this very same fact appears almost obvious. No dreamer (actually, no human being) could regard as a nightmare any dream in which everything was light, bright and lofty. Every dreamer (and thus every human being, either asleep or awake) would appreciate lightness, brightness, and a lofty atmosphere to be characteristics of a beautiful dream. These characteristics evoke such unanimous appreciation, in the eyes of any and every dreamer that they seem to have an "objective" existence of their own. Any person who has ever dreamt a dream in which these characteristics appeared would recognize on every such occasion that without these characteristics the dream would lose its beauty. Moreover, without them, the very process of dreaming the dreamt beauty would be lost. One would be drawn to the conclusion that these characteristics are the "pillars" which sustain the world exposed by a beautiful dream. Thus, lightness, brightness, and loftiness have a reality in and of themselves, without which this whole world would collapse and disintegrate. It is as if the characteristics of a beautiful dream were a "thing" that one could hold in one's hand. They can be considered as the only real "thing" in the illusion of a dream. They appear in the dream as the "real" presence of the illusion, which allows the illusion of the dream to be "really" dreamt.

Being disabled I observe the dream state to have an inherent tendency of discrimination: I find in a dream an intrinsic capacity to have an effect upon itself and thus to shape itself. I believe that a dream has an influence upon itself through producing a discrimination between

Re-organization of bones

After the death of Feldenkrais I took Jonathan once or twice a
year to lecture in front of the Feldenkrais instructors course. I took
him out to the car to the lecture room and back. It took Jhonathan
about an hour to arrange his bones and body after each change in
place. Organizing his bones was very important to Jonathan, in
order to prevent respiratory problems due to asthma.

Danny

Stretching Jonathan

I came to hear a lecture. I didn't know a thing about the speaker's
disability. The hall on Bnei-Dan Street was packed. Suddenly
someone shoved a wheelchair into the room and put it in the front
row facing the audience. In the wheelchair I saw a little cramped
man. Much to my surprise, this man began to talk about something
that needed to be done for him, something unpleasant. It was
made clear, that if someone was not comfortable with the sight,
they could leave the room. Then, the therapist started to stretch
and pull him in his chair. He moved his head and stretched it out,
and then moved limb by limb. I was shocked. The sight was very
difficult to watch. Some people left the Hall. I felt repugnance, but
I stayed. Within a few minutes a full pledged man was sitting on
the chair with his head set high.

Dorit Givon

two distinct sets of its very own characteristics. Dreams have a selective impact upon their horizontal and vertical characteristics. The horizontal characteristics of a dream would be blurred out, so that its vertical characteristics could be intensely highlighted.

This "selective" tendency of dreams to undermine their own horizontal characteristics through emphasizing their vertical ones, can be found in nightmares as well. This inherent increase in the "weight" that vertical facts have in proportion to the horizontal ones is present in nightmares not less than in beautiful dreams. A nightmare seems to place special importance on "dark" occurrences (which take the dreamer away from the sun through forcing him to dwell in the "lower" domains of reality). A nightmare, on other occasions, would attribute significance to its own "heave" characteristics (which drag the dreamer into lower regions of the world). There are nightmares that would even design the scenery in which their plot takes place in a series of trenches, cellars, and subway tunnels.

When going to sleep one would naturally expect to awaken in the bed in which the dreaming process had been taking place. Similarly whenever I think ahead of what is about to take place with me, it is natural for me to expect my paralysis to maintain its position in the bed to which I am confined. The point I am trying to make is that my paralyzed body has a stillness which resembles the stillness of a dreaming person. The difference, however, between myself as disabled and a dreaming person as still, is that the world of a dreaming person is clearly split between inner and outer events. Thus, the dream is occurring only inside the dreaming person, whilst outside the stillness

Shifting to the perfect position

John learned to activate us out of the understanding that without help from friends he won't be able to proceed. Therefore, he taught us not to be ashamed to touch him, treat him, shift and move him. He was an excellent teacher, and we learned to sit him on his wheelchair, lay him in bed, put him in the car and take him out of the car, adjust his head, move his feet and lift his shoulder – until it all came to the perfect position for him. It was a routine activity, but sometimes when we were doing it on the street, people were watching and thought we just came off the moon.

Gadi Ravnitzki

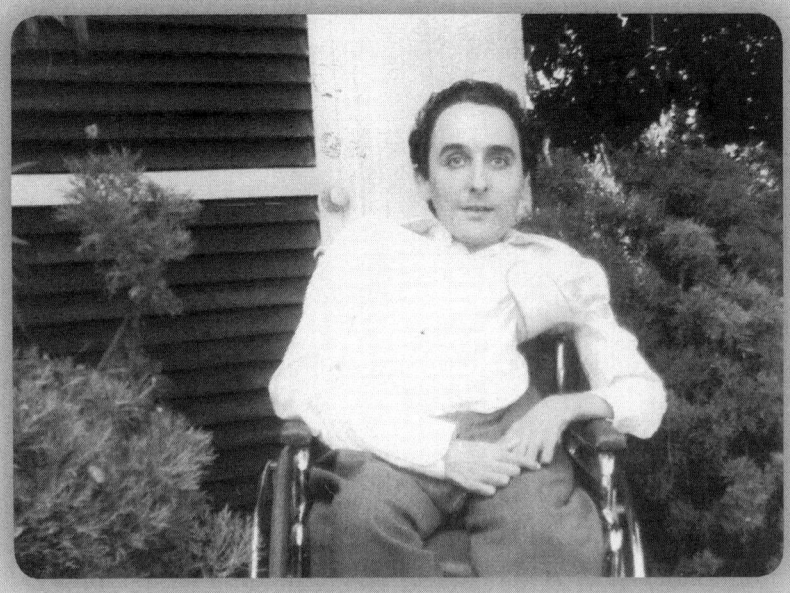

Jonathan, 1982

of the sleeping body is imbedded in everyday reality. In contrast to this, the view I hold of the world as filtered through my paralysis takes place on the very same plane as the immobility of my bedridden body.

When I consider dreams from the perspective I have because of my disability, I am struck by several facts. The first astonishing fact is: If dreams hold within themselves an extra meaning that everyday reality lacks (a nightmare has a "negative" extra meaning, whilst a beautiful dream has an extra meaning which is positive), where does this extra meaning come from? From where do we extract this additional meaning that dreams have, if this richer meaning does not exist in everyday reality? If this extra meaning is not taken from everyday reality (which is "too poor" to contain it), then from what is it taken or from where does it come to us in sleep? The second fact concerning dreams that seems unexplained to me is the following: a person, whilst dreaming, is not only still (not only lying motionless, usually in bed), but is also unaware of his/her stillness. If dreaming is connected to a stillness of the body, how come this stillness does not leave its mark on the dream itself, and how come the connection between physical stillness and dreaming does not manifest itself in the dream. In short, why does the dream not disclose the fact that the dreamer is still?

The third problematic aspect of dreaming which occurred to me seems to me to be a kind of reversed version of the second question. At times we do experience a "dream-like" state, of which we are very much aware. We all feel at one time or another that life has become so beautiful that it

Move it here, move it there

Sometimes Jonathan was very burdensome. For example, when working with him, he would say: "now elbow, ok, Im moving my elbow, now I'm moving to the other side, now the elbow..." At some point I told him: "tell me it's wrong when it is wrong, and ok when it's right". Then he turned to the other side. And it could take, I do not know... about 20 minutes. And at the end: move over here, move over there. He was very aware of his sensory system. If I held his elbow in my right hand – he would ask me to hold it in my left hand. He had quite a lot of criticism about what had happened to the Feldenkrais method today, how it became commercialized. He always used to tell me: we need to talk about it. Half of the classes he was asleep. Every time I worked on his right side he slept. The truth was that I fell asleep as well, since the room was heated even at August. I always had to fight with him. I tried to persuade Danny to cheat him with the heat. He turned on the heat in order to dry the towels or whatever. They did me a special favor and lowered the heat and opened the window a little so I could have some fresh air. In short, it was stifling in the room, and I fell asleep again and again. Jonathan fell asleep as usual, maybe a little more than usual, but it seemed normal to me. In his last year I didn't feel his deterioration. And then one day I received an e-mail from Michael informing me that Jonathan died. We were supposed to have a class together the next day.

Benny Chor

somehow "transcends" itself and becomes a "dream-come-true". On other occasions we find that life "transcends" itself in an unhappy direction, and has become a "nightmare". If these very happy and very unhappy conditions do indeed have something in common with the state of dreaming in sleep, why unlike dreaming in sleep are they not obviously connected to a state of physical stillness? Why does a "dream-come-true" or a "nightmare" manifest in everyday reality not display any real associations with stillness, and why can it take place in an everyday reality that seems to have very little to do with stillness? In short, how come it makes any sense to all to call such occasions a "dream-come-true" or a "nightmare"?

I tried to see if I could answer the first question through applying certain experiences derived from my disability. In its original form I put to myself this first question as asking: from where does the extra beauty or the extra horror found only in dreams come to us? Whilst pondering this difficulty from a disabled person's point of view, I noticed a new fact. Dreams always spring from a very special context. Before dreaming (and after it) we all need to go through a phase of "deathlike" experience, which we call dreamless sleep. In other words, we need to supply ourselves with a void-like context, which alone can contain our peak impressions of beauty (in the form of a beautiful dream) and horror (in the form of a nightmare). Outside this blank arena of dreamless sleep there exists no other context from which dreaming can come forth. This exclusiveness of the context of sleep proves to be problematic when we consider another fact: everything that we know in the world is held

The sense of body

I belong to a group of people who Feldenkrais himself taught and trained in order to continue his path. After Mia left to Japan, I started working with Jonathan. For me it was complete shock. You walk in and you meet… What do you do with such a person? A man whose head is in one place, his shoulder in another, legs, foot, ribs… What law of nature do you work with? With gravity, skeletal muscle? No. You work with the human being himself. I met a man who told me what exactly he wants and needs. It was one of the great things that have happened to me: I became the recipient. He told me: I want to feel what it's like to walk. I never walked in my entire life, and I just want to feel what it's like. How do you give a man who spends his life lying down the sense of walking?

Part of the Feldenkrais theory and method is giving a person the feeling of the foot. But the amazing thing about Jonathan was that he was talking about feeling, about senses. He was able to identify each part of his body, until at some point he said:"yes, I can feel the floor!" It was astonishing to see how a person can feel the artificial floor through his own guidance, and not only through the sensitivity of my hands. This is just a little story that changed part of my work with people with disabilities. I learned what disability is in terms of personality, not only disability of the body. It was very important to Jonathan to participate in each class I taught about how he understood and experienced the Feldenkrais method – in order to give people knowledge and understanding how to understand Feldenkrais method differently through disability. Thus he came to every class I taught and told people his story. One of the amazing stories he told was about the difference between leading a stone or leading a person. When one leads a stone, he dos not need to consider where he walks, if he walks on a crooked floor or stepping on to the sidewalk. But in space – our family, our neighbors, our belongings, the city in which we live and the entire cosmos all fit in the "container" we call space. Furthermore, if we are looking for any of these items – for example, a location of which we have the address or a friend living in that location – we would turn to the space around us, knowing that only there, in that "container" can anything be found. Yet, the striking fact is that space fails to provide us with dreams. Experience shows that space in not capable of holding within itself anything which is not tangible or real. This limitation is what governs the ability of space to serve us. Therefore, the deathlike hollowness of sleep has to be the one and only container which can possibly provide us with dreams. Indeed, when falling asleep we seem to be making a choice between the two possible containers: we choose to reject space in favor of sleep. In short, going to sleep entails a replacement of space by a slumber-like state serving as a "container" of dreams. Bearing this conclusion in mind, I was clear about one thing: the extra beauty and the extra horror found in dreams come in the "container" of sleep, and can come only in this container. However, there still remains another unsolved issue: How do this extra beauty and extra horror exist in the "sleep" container? Where did they originate before entering sleep? From where did sleep derive its dreamt contents?

I tried to tackle these questions, allowing my paralyzed condition to produce its own answer for me. I felt how my paralysis prevents me from making any real "use" of the space in which I am contained. What I undergo as a disabled person is an experience that although space is all when one leads a man, he must constantly look around and see what is around him – because any turmoil has a aching effect on the person you lead. Two or three years ago I broke my leg and was in a wheelchair. Only then I realized what he really felt. There were only a few people Jonathan enabled to lead him, to push his wheelchair. Then I noticed the difference between the feeling of the person sitting in the wheelchair and the feeling of the person pushing the wheelchair.

Chava Shelhav

Instructors course

Jonathan wanted to be involved in endowing Feldenkrais method and sought to deepen his knowledge in it and introduce it to new trainees. In the beginning of his career as a Feldenkrais teacher, when Jonathan still had the ability to speak, I helped him meet students and talk to them during or after an instructors course.

Lior Pessach

Personal guidence

Jonathan wanted to introduce the Feldenkrais method to as many as he could. He attributed to Feldenkrais the fact that his life was prolonged Significantiy- much more than the average of his disease. Jonathan bellived that if children were taught Feldenkrais at school at a young age, a generation of children would grow up healthy in body and spirit.

Shosh Foyerlicht

around me, I cannot move in it or through it by myself. Since I concluded that there are only two "container" (emptiness, i.e. space, and void, i.e. dreamless sleep), it followed that paralysis places me in the second "container" – in the sleep-like world. Although this conclusion may seem strange (since paralysis does not put me to sleep), it reflects my experience.

I felt that, indeed, disability allows me to live in a condition that resembles at least in some ways, that of sleep. Yet, I also felt that the inert state of my system, in other ways, goes beyond the range of experience, and even of peak experiences, offered by dreams.

When I felt my way in trying to solve this difficulty, a certain clue presented itself, which I ascribed to the sense produced in me by my physical condition. A possible link, which I had not thought of until then, now occurred to me as a bridge connecting the two "containers": On the one hand, the void of the sleeping condition, and on the other hand, the space of the awakened state, now, for the first time, seemed to be interconnected. It struck me that in any one of my dreams, many different chains of events, and a whole variety of known and unknown human characters were involved. I dreamt of high-school teachers I encountered in the remote past, of cities I wanted to visit all my life without being able to do so, and of unthinkable and absurd situations which were occurring in the spur of the moment. Then I decided to play a mental game with my dreams. I imagined myself reaching out with one of my hands into the world of a dream, whilst I was in the process of dreaming it. I pictured my hand picking out

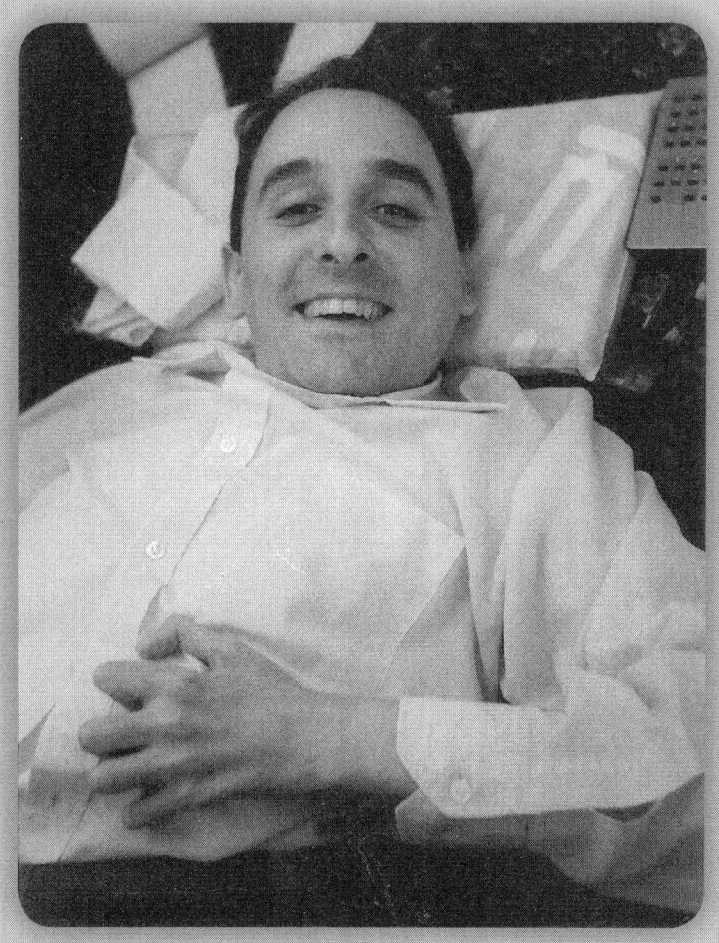

Jonathan, 1986

Assistance

Yonatan asked for help in regard to several things, and in this way set up a network of help, which continued up until the day he died. He managed all of the the friends and volunteers by himself.

Uri Nissel

a certain character, and trying to pull the character out from the dream in order to bring it into the real world. I saw in my mind's eye that my hand would soon discover that this character was made of "nothingness" – it was a "void character", which would immediately disappear into thin air. I carried on with my game, envisioning my hand seizing one by one additional characters, and even several objects, all of which were participating in the very same dream. Again, my imagination seemed to lead me to the same realization: as my hand was clutching any ingredient of my dream,(either one of the living characters or a particular inanimate item) the same process repeated itself with every additional try. As more and more details of my dream seemed to be transformed from a "thing" to a "nothing" their secret was being found out. The nature of them all was now proving to have been void – like from the very start.

A curious relationship between the void (sleep) and space (reality) was being unveiled by the mental game I was playing. In my game my hand was emerging from the space of reality in order to "transgress" into the void of sleep. It was doing so when reaching out to grasp the items and examine their nature. It made sense to envisage my hand "crossing the border line" running between reality and sleep, since my hand's position in space was being maintained during this entire process, (my hand was traversing the edge of reality's space only in order to enter upon my dream's space). All that was required of my hand was to move from one space to another, and therefore it seemed reasonable to expect my hand to be capable of performing the task

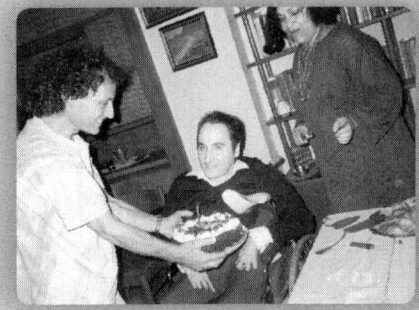
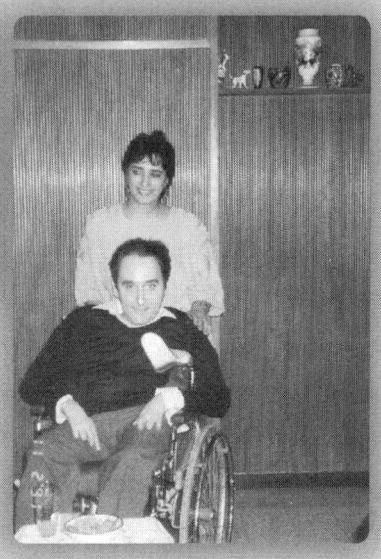

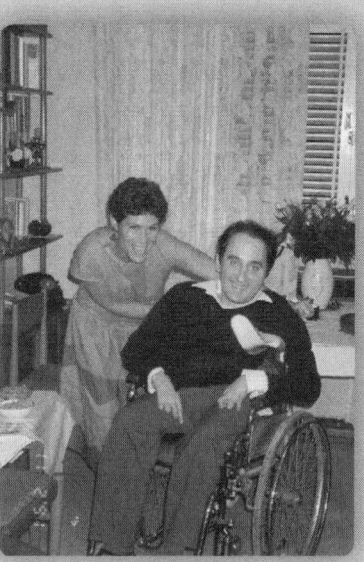

Fortieth Birthday, 1991

I allotted to it (to scan my dreams). Both in reality and in sleep, all that was being required from my hand was to move itself in space. Yet, a striking difference between the two spaces then occurred to me. The "real" space my hand was traversing was capable of containing everything in the world except from "the stuff of which dreams are made of". This "stuff" could be found nowhere in reality and thus it was quite obvious that the space of reality was not suitable to hold within itself such stuff. It seemed that such stuff needed a special space which reality failed to provide. The space inside the dream was also a space which encompassed a complete world – the world of a dream in its entirety. However, this space was capable of holding within itself a world of items, characters, objects, etc. that were all made of "nothingness". This space was very different from the space outside the dream. In contrast to the space outside the dream in which no stuff of which dreams are made of could be held, the space inside the dream had capabilities that were almost diametrically opposed. The dream space had the unique gift for just that – to serve as a container for the "nothingness" of which dreams are made.

This special space of a dream had an additional unique characteristic – it could be attained only after falling asleep and before waking up. Thus the dream space could appear only within a special context characterized by its death-like blankness (usually called dreamless sleep). Before my game I assumed the dreams to be simply hanging around separately, just anywhere in the void. But now through playing my game I realized that they were restricted to a specific location within the larger void. Dreams were

Wheelchair dancing

I met Jonathan at Moshe and Sarah's wedding. I arrived late and waited outside the hall. I was advised to sit near the bar in front of the elevator so I could see the people coming from the chuppa. The first to appear was my friend Henry Unger pushing Jonathan's wheelchair. He introduced me to Johnathan, and by the time we sat at the table to eat it was as if we were friends for many years. Jonathan, known as Joker, could soften the awkward first moments with humor and laughter. His disability was very obvious, but his cheerfulness and friendliness hid the feeling of compassion people naturally felt. The first thought that accompanied me on my return home was that I had just met a very unique individual and that I am very fortunate. During the wedding party, a lively conversation took place around the table. When the dancing began I dared and invited Jonathan to dance with me. To my joy, Jonathan accepted my invitation warmly, an invitation which was a new experience for me. The extraordinary experience of the wheelchair dance with Jonathan felt to me like the most natural thing to do.

Only the next day did I realized how special the experience was for Jonathan as well. He called me the next morning to thank me for the special experience. "Through the movment of the wheels I felt as if my feet are moving," he said. That first phone conversation, which lasted for three hours, was the beginning of the process of my understanding that physical disability is just one angle of the story. Until then I didn't know someone in a similar situation. I realized that physical feelings and experiences are so clear and obvious to me, while Jonathan felt these feelings through his imagination and the instincts that he developed for himself. Only then did I realize how important and special was my dance invitation to him.

Shosh Foyerlicht

restricted to make their appearance in a definite space –
the space of a dream. Thus the case proved to be as follows:
When studying the nature of the void (a container) I
found it to hold within it another container (the space of
a dream). Only within this last container (which itself was
contained within the void) could a dream exist. Therefore,
a dream appeared solely when enveloped by a container
(space) which itself existed as the internal aspect of an
additional external container (void). In short, a dream
existed only when encompassed by two concentric layers
of containers (a space within a void).

At this point I attempted to play another game with myself.
I wondered whether the space of a dream and the void of
sleep could be divorced from one another. I toyed with the
idea of putting to use each of these two containers as a
special arena having its independent effect upon a given
portion of the world. The purpose of my initiative was to
try to transport each container separately into the world
around me. I anticipated the outcome of introducing what
had been my notion of the void of sleep to the reality I was
aware of while being awake. I expected that such a joining
of the vividness of waking reality with the blankness of
sleep would result in an experience similar to the one I
had as a disabled person. However, before examining my
paralyzed state through the application of such a procedure
I decided to turn to the other element comprising my new
game. I wanted to check first what would happen when I
transported the space of my dreams into the space of the
reality in which I lived. As I tried doing so I realized that
there was nothing new in my attempt. I had always known

At the wedding of Sarah and Moshe Blacher

how to "imagine", and "day-dream" or "fantasize". When "envisioning" anything, I needed to make use of "space", (i.e. the space in which images appear when I conjured them in my wakened state) and place this "space" within the context of my everyday reality. My day dreaming could occur only in a kind of "crystal ball" (a closed portion of space held within the bounds of my everyday life). This "crystal ball" (imagination) would serve me a secluded arena, in which I alone could decide which images would be conjured up from nowhere or disappear at will into thin air. The fantasized events that took place within the "crystal ball" stood in sharp contrast with those that occurred outside of it – in the everyday reality all around. Everything that belonged to reality could not disappear and reappear at a whim. Yet, I could daydream only for as long as my "crystal ball" continued to produce its "magical" effects in the very midst of the everyday realm: Were my "crystal ball" to lose its position in the very midst of the every-day realm, then I would no longer be "day-dreaming" but rather "night-dreaming". When "visualizing" in this way (i.e. when staying awake) I was actually carrying the "dream-space" out of its original context out of the void of sleep – and transporting this "dream-space" into the reality surrounding my everyday awakened state. I noticed that the dream space maintained its own special properties even after having been uprooted from its place in sleep and transplanted into the real world. These special properties could only have been acquired by the dream space through its earlier association with the void of sleep. I was surprised by how my capacity to "imagine" (to produce "dreams" in everyday reality) was molded by the

Sara Blacher and Shosh Foierlicht congratulate Jonathan
on his fortieth birthday

With friends on his fortieth birthday, 1991

void of sleep, in that my imagination was at its best when it functioned along "vertical" lines. I could best imagine things when the things I imagined were of a high-low (or up-down) inclination. My imagination would direct itself "upwards" when I introduced my own ideals and values into the everyday world. Whenever I needed to set "high" standards in planning my future course of activity (to choose for myself objectives of a "lofty" nature, I found myself turning to my imagination (the "crystal ball"). My imagination, and only my imagination, could introduce from out of nowhere standards "higher" than reality itself, and aims that would serve to bring everyday life to "loftier" purposes. Thus, my "crystal ball" obviously did possess an "up" (or "high") dimension – its positive polarity. Similarly, my imagination would almost automatically be mobilized for my use, whenever I dreaded or feared something (especially when such an anxiety would become almost "phobic"). Hallucinations, by their very nature, could only stem from a dream-like context. They were not real and thus could only belong in a "dream space". However, once such "dreams" became either real fears or even "phobias", they would be taken out of their original dream context, and would be now situated in the midst of everyday occurrences. Consequently, on such occasions, my imagination would have an impact on the reality of my everyday conduct. My imagination would then disclose its "negative" polarity – that of dragging me "down", to a level "lower" than the real world. I came to the conclusion that whenever my "dream space" was put to use as "imagination" (i.e. placed in the outside world) it would make its way in order to reach either "beyond" reality (when revealing its "upward" inclination)

Sightseeing

Shoshi Foyerlicht and Sarah Blacher would take Jonathan for walks near the Yarkon river. Only specific friends were allowed to take Jonatan on these walks. They took him to the Tel Aviv Museum as well. In the museum they would often stop by differant paintings and have a discussion about them. They were constantly traveling, going to concerts, movies, and most of all – to exhibitions at the Museum. There, Jonatan's artistic insight was at almost mystical proportions. Jonathan loved to see movies and loved to hear concerts. Sarah and Jonathan were on the phone for hours at a time. When Jonathan had an idea, he simply called her and asked her to write it down for him.

From an interview.

or "below" reality (when the tendency disclosed was pointing "downward"). In short, reality seemed to fail to condense its "horizontality" into the "vertical" dimension that the "dream space" would bring with it. The "dream space", when transformed into awakened imagination, seemed to impose upon the "horizontality" of reality, a "vertical" nature, which had originated in the "void" of sleep. As I reflected upon this process, I realized what I was really doing, in order to set the "dream space" within its new arena of reality. When doing so, I had no choice but to create a distinct division between the space I was translocating ("the dream space"), and the void of sleep (which remained in its original environment). A "split" occurred, and as a result the "void" of sleep on the one hand, and the "dream space" on the other, were being kept apart from each other.

I wanted to carry on with my new game and toying with the "void of sleep". My game had involved so far only the "dream space" – that space that contains "the stuff of which dreams are made". I wanted my game to move into a further stage. I desired to include in my game that "nothingness" that everyone goes through when falling asleep without dreaming. My intention was to try and play with dreamless sleep (the blank context). I wanted to toy with this blankness (or nothingness) of sleep, and to try to make use of it in my life. When I was "experimenting" with the "dream space", I had done so by "transporting" it from inside my dream into the outside space of reality. I ended up with what I coined "the crystal ball" of imagination. All this had happened when I was playing with "the stuff of which dreams are made". I was now planning the new

אוניברסיטת תל-אביב

רקטור האוניברסיטה

ודקאן הפקולטה למדעי הרוח ע״ש לסטר וסאלי אנטין

מעניקים

למר **יונתן כהן**

את התואר

מוסמך
אוניברסיטה (M.A.)

בפילוסופיה

לאחר שסיים את חוק לימודיו

בהצטיינות יתרה

והגיש עבודת גמר

תל-אביב, י״ח בסיון תשס״ו, 14 ביוני 2006

פרופ׳ שלמה בידרמן

הדקאן

פרופ׳ דני ליתן

הרקטור

Jonathan Kahan, Tel Aviv University M.Sc. cum laude in Philosophy

phase of the game. I asked myself whether anything that originated in the outside world could be launched in the form of a "crystal ball" and end up landing in the "void of sleep". I was curious to see if it were possible to introduce into the "void of sleep" something that did not originate inside it (such as a dream) but instead had originated outside it – something that would enter the "void of sleep" coming directly from the outside world. I assumed that such a quest might result in my finding an additional "crystal ball". The kind of "crystal ball" I was seeking would travel from the rich complexity of the world I was aware of outside of me and aim at entering the total blankness of my world of sleep.

It then occurred to me what such a "crystal ball" might prove to be. I thought of the nature of an organism whence sleeping. Everything in the organism is designed for its movement in space – in the outside world. The ankles, knees, calves, and even the small of the back and the nape of the neck are all fashioned in a way that allows them to work with space – to move themselves from one place to another in the outside world. In other words, for as long as the members of an organism are outside the void, they exist as a means of exploring space. However, from the moment they enter the void they no longer follow their original purpose of translocating the organism. Yet, even when imbedded in the void of sleep, the members of the body maintain their original moving design despite that fact that they no longer move. They lose their capacity to direct themselves to additional locations in space, and yet they maintain the design that is required to do just that. This moving structure now seems to bring about the presence of

The healthiest of men

I learned so much from him. Sometimes people come to me and say this hurts, that hurts, and then I tell them about the healthiest man I ever knew. I tell them about Yonatan. He was really the healthiest man I ever knew. He lived a full and complete life.

Mia Segal

Jonathan, 1990

sleep. This configuration becomes the framework in which sleep "settles in". Sleep can be present only in an organism whose design serves a double purpose: the organism's design must allow it either to function through moving in space – when it is awake – or to be immersed in the total blankness of stillness – when it sleeps. We all seem to use only a single set of members and organs (we do not have more than one body) yet this single organism can reveal its stillness through being asleep, or else reveal its very own movement through being awake. Thus our physicality can either be "embodied" in the blankness of the void or else "incorporated" in the reality of space.

It thus became clear that the human body was endowed with a capacity to involve itself in either one of the "containers" – either in the void or in space. Indeed, as I paid more attention to my own body, I noticed it had both a "space reality" (for as long as it was awake) and a "void reality" (for as long as it was asleep). I saw that for as long as my body realized itself as a "space reality" it consisted of a three-dimensional organism. This "spatial" self-realization of my body existed in the form of joints, bones and muscles – it existed as a means for movement. By contrast, when my body realized itself as a "void reality" (as opposed to a "space reality"), everything about it existed as the total blankness of dreamless sleep. In this "sleep realization" all my organs, my muscles, my bones, my joints, etc. (including all movement that could occur through my members) were united as an unbroken void. Thus, instead of appearing in space, my body would disappear into complete blankness for as long as it was asleep. In short, when my body realized itself in space it would appear, and when it realized itself as a void it would disappear.

Who will take care of him?

Once we had a conversation about his disease and what would happen after his mother passed away. What and where he would be.

Yonatan said: I could never go anywhere else. I will remain at home. You [Ina] and Danny and Tina will have to take care of me.

He didn't want to go to an institution because he was afraid of illness and disease. He learned how to manage on his own. Once, when he was checking out a certain institution, he told them his requirements. They said there was no way they could care for him; that according to his requirements, his care would require the work of 15 people.

Ina the Caregiver

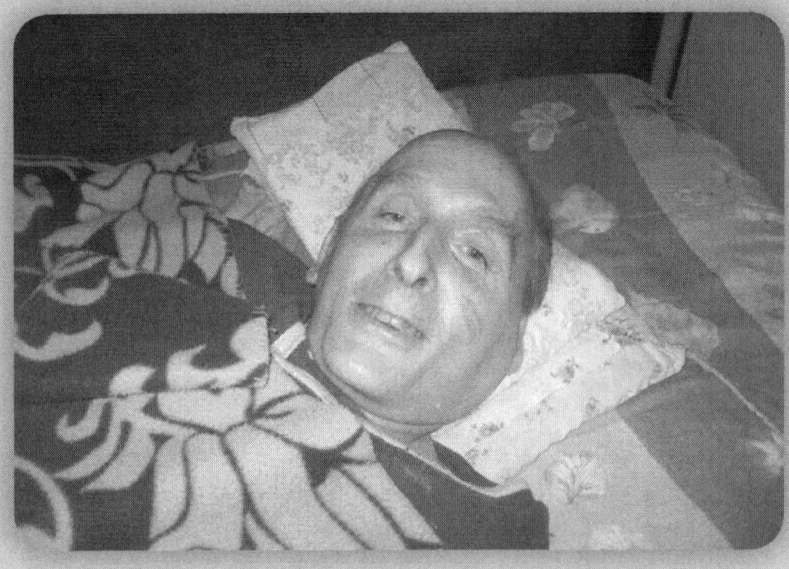

Smile to life at sixty birthday, two weeks before his death

There still was an issue that remained unclear: how did my body "launch" itself from the space outside into the void of sleep? In other words, how could my body "transport" itself from the arena of movement (space) into the arena of sleep (the void)? As I observed my body I saw that it could "catapult" itself from space to void by eliminating its own appearance (and thus disappear into the void). It could eliminate its own appearance (and thus "catapult" itself into the void) through bringing about the disappearance of space. I felt that the disappearance of space was the means by which my body "launched" itself into the world of sleep.

I gave much thought to my new way of evaluating the human body. I was surprised at the possibility of discovering more aspects of our physical life. It was obvious that our body's involvement in space allowed it an almost endless range of possibilities. I know that through using its existence in space, the human body could hold books and read them, could view TV screens at a distance or hear music in a specially designed hall; the body could also run, leap, jump, sit down, drive a car or even travel to the moon – and the list has only begun! What excited me was the prospect of involving the body in an additional "container" – the "void" of sleep. Would such an additional involvement entail additional, almost endless potential?

It seems reasonable to suppose that evidence of such a potential could be found even in the Darwinian theory of evolution. One could ask why sleep was not eliminated in the course of evolution. Do no long hours of sleep expose any living creature to the danger of attacking predators? Three and a half billion years of evolution have allowed life to develop the most sophisticated mechanisms – on

Anna at her home, September 2013

land, under water and in the air. Evolution has brought into being almost unthinkable strategies for survival. How is it, then, that the fittest who survived were not creatures who did not need to waste such a large part of their lives in sleep? One does not need to stretch one's imagination in order to conjure up the image of creatures who could "store up" energy and yet remain awake and vigilant. Since the apparent aspects of sleep seem to entail only obvious disadvantages, it occurred to me that sleep might actually hold some hitherto unthought-of benefits. In pursuing this line of thought, I came to the conclusion that we might all be unaware of what sleep truly offers us.

Equipment and administration

I was responsible for the technical subjects such as programming and maintenance of a special remote control device – by which Jonathan was able to trigger and use the TV, tape recorder, video, cables, etc. It was a small device that was placed on Jonathan's cheek, and Jonathan used his one finger which still had some capacity. I filled special requests of his, such as buying books of Japanese and Chinese paintings from museums around the world. Since Jonathan slept most of the day in front of one wall, he ordered his assistants to hang on the wall some of these paintings, which made changing and multicolored exhibition. In addition, I also bought different electrical appliances according to special settings and orders that Jonathan maintained. Jonathan was very meticulous, and so buying an electrical appliance was accompanied by in-depth market research, multiple tests preformed by different friends and great indecisions until the final ruling. From any device that was purchased, a spare identical device was purchased as well in fear of the future where this device will not be available any more. Since Jonathan's room was small, he asked friends to hold the spare devices in their homes for him. In the past ten years – after his mother stopped taking care of Financial Affairs – I helped Jonathan manage his bank accounts and handled administrative matters. Jonathan didn't use modern means of Internet and telephone orders and needed help in monitoring the accounts, payments and more.

Uri Nissel

CHAPTER 5

SPACE AND THE VOID

I observed two distinct "containers" in which my life was taking place: One was the "horizontality" of space (which allowed movement to exist) and the other was the "verticality" of stillness (best portrayed by the "void" of dreamless sleep). There existed, however, an additional issue, which I hadn't yet thoroughly studied: What is the relationship that prevails between space and the void? Where is their meeting place or where is the "crossroads" where they "intersect"? At first, I did not know how to cope with the problem this represented. It was only when I turned to my disability that I could clearly detect the "bridge" which joined the domains of space and the void. I could find the "common ground" of both only when I regarded the issue from my personal vantage point – from within my paralyzed condition.

Since I could never walk or even stand upon my legs, I chose to study my disability by focusing specifically upon the condition of my lower limbs. As I grew more attentive

Specific orders

One of my Specific tasks was to put the envelopes in the room and write on each envelope its contents. When I started caring for Jonathan, I didn't know Hebrew well enough, so I wrote in English and with no special attention. Jonathan asked me to write in neat hand-writing. Once I asked him: what will you do with all these envelopes? What do you need all the replicas for? And Jonathan answered: it is important to me, and I want it done. Every morning I knew what I had to do: organize the envelopes, make replicas, and then deel with the phone calls and other things. The envelopes had to be put on the shelf in specific order according to Jonathan's instructions. If Danny was around I had to close the door so he wouldn't see. Gideon would bring Annie money to pay the caregivers. The money was in her control, and she didn't like it. Nevertheless, she took care of all the money issues until she had no ability to continue, and then Jonathan began to run everything by himself. He learned how to handle all the chores at home. I took care of all the writing issues, but I didn't actually write myself. There were recordings and folders. When his problems began, when he stopped writing – he had no energy. Jonathan didn't want people who didn't understand what he wrote to deal with his writings.

Ina the caregiver

to the nature of my paralysis, I noticed a strange fact. All the parts of my legs (the heels, ankles, calves, knees and thighs) possessed the design (or shape) specially needed for standing up and walking. Upon my legs was "imprinted" (or "carved") the kind of shape that would imply only one thing – standing and walking, yet the paralysis of these very same legs implied the exact opposite – the non-presence precisely of either standing or walking. Despite the fact that I was always bedridden and standing and walking were never accomplished, the inborn design of my legs was maintained throughout my personal history. In other words, because of my malady, the structures needed for standing and walking could never be put to use by me, and yet they were at all times fully present. For as long as my legs existed (and they existed all the time, despite my disability) they became a physical (or material) indication of the unavailability of movement. Inasmuch as my legs were part of me, they served as living evidence to the missing ability for which they were destined. Thus the role played by my lower limbs had been transformed through my physical condition. All that the reality of my legs did in my life was to point to the total absence of my standing and my walking. Thus the presence of paralysis served as an unavoidable reminder to the non-presence of the role normally played by legs.

Was the presence of my legs not disclosing to me a design for walking, I would not have felt myself to be a disabled person. My being disabled meant to me that I had lost an ability that I was due to possess (standing and walking). In other words I felt my disability as an ability whose existence belonged to my nature but that

The collection of reproductions of Jonathan, photo 2013

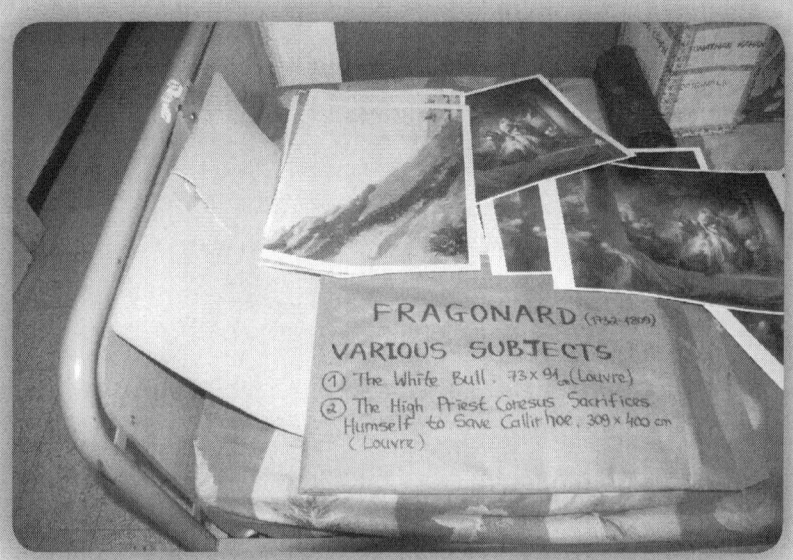

The artwork in Jonathan's room, photo 2013

was nevertheless taken away from me. It was an ability I naturally had, and then lost for one reason or another. In short, I had the experience of a loss – a loss of ability, and hence a "dis-ability". Consequently, paralysis was an everlasting presence which was turning my attention to an everlasting absence. The constant absence of standing and walking gave me through my legs, an unusual sensation: not the sensation of something that is, but the sensation of something that is not. Strangely, it was a direct feeling of a missing presence, the sense of a void in the very solidity of my legs. It was an experience of a void that could be found only when looked for through my legs. In no way was the void mental – its sensation was completely physical, since I felt it not in my mind nor through my mind, but rather in my body and through my body. In short, it was my paralysis that made this void accessible to my mind.

The void I felt through my disability resembled in many ways the void I was used to feel when sleeping. Both had a "nothingness" flavor to them and both seemed to exist without time and hence ousted of time. Both "voids" (that of sleep and that of disability) were similar in this aspect – they both displayed the same non-relation to time, and I experience indeed this non-relation that they displayed as a complete "nothingness". However, I sensed an unmistakable difference between the void of sleep and the void of disability. The difference between the two "voids" did not prevail in their non-relationship to time, but rather in a different relation to space. The void of sleep existed outside space – not only was it radically divorced from the space of the world which surrounded sleep, but it was also clearly set apart from the space of my dreams.

Jonathan's room tapes, photo 2013

Dreams did occur in sleep, but the space in which they happened was distinctly held outside the void of sleep. The void of sleep embraced all of my dreams, and yet never appeared within them. I observed that the void of sleep had as little relationship to space as it had to time. The void of disability, by contrast, held a distinct relationship with space. For one thing I found this void only after I had turned to space. I needed to scan the space that my body occupied before I could pinpoint those places where paralysis "opened up" its space to the void dimension.

My knee was transmitting to me its three-dimensional structure in space. What was thus conveyed to my perception was the precise volume that my knee occupied. I had a vivid impression of the contrasts presented by its different surfaces (its front, its back, etc.). I felt that my knee was not fashioned in space, according to an arbitrary design. Quite the opposite. It demonstrated a very specific structure – that structure required for bending and straightening. Its unchanging shape was as frozen in space as my paralysis. However, despite its inert configuration, my knee's form was that of an organ destined to bend and straighten itself. It was thus disclosing "secrets" and "hints" about the nature of walking. My knee's special presence demonstrated to me that a walking organ must preserve the space dimension of its own movement, even if it has lost the capacity to move. Consequently, only through introducing to me its own spatial presence could my knee transmit to me the fact that both bending and straightening required the space medium. My leg could straighten only in space, and it similarly required the very same space in order to bend itself. Thus bending and

Milbat

I first met Jonathan at his home in Tel Aviv. His mother opened the door and led me to his room. I met a little man, covered in a thick blanket, a nice-looking face with burning eyes, a sharp and alert look. The little room was packed with crowds of music cassettes arranged on the shelves. On the surrounding walls were pictures of art pinned to a magnetic board which enabled replacement. All objects in the room were arranged in an exemplary manner. I came to Jonathan with a small electric switch which he asked Milbat to install. At this stage of his life he regularly was in his bed and was able to move only one finger on each hand.

I started to build him a small surface with switches for maximizing his left hand hand finger movement and enable him to run three separate systems.

This was the beginning of a relationship of many years. In each one of my visits I added according to his requests additional options. After a while he had a complete music system, and it served him to play classical music.

Most important was the telephone system. At first he was totally dependent on his Filipino assistant in all telephonic communications. Once I built a system with a microphone hanging over his head, he could answer and call any one of his many friends. In this way he managed to run his life. The same system allowed him to control lighting and heatingin the room and open the door. All this by verbal commands. to

For many years I had close contact with Jonathan and responded to all requests. I was impressed by his strength of mind and vast intellectual ability to live a full life.

Zeev Schmidt

straightening would be unfamiliar to me were my knee not to exist in the medium, which would afford such activity – space. However, bending and straightening were not at all to be found in my leg because of my malady, and yet both could clearly be sensed because of the spatial structure of my knee. Thus, whilst the physical ability to straighten and bend was absent in my knee, what remained intact in my knee was the spatial nature of bending and straightening, and this spatial nature alone. So that the dimension of space, and dimension alone, remained present in my knee as the one and only aspect which allowed this paralyzed member to remain a "knee", despite its motionlessness.

My knee, were it a normally functioning organ, would have involved my system in far more than spatial activity. Were my knee not disabled, it would have involved both my calf and my thigh in a conspicuous repertoire of movement. However, my knee being as paralyzed as it was, maintained the usual involvement that such an organ must have with space, but was unable to produce any movement either (for) the calf or thigh. Instead, what I felt through my knee, both in my calf and in my thigh, was an absence of movement – a void that permeated these parts of me, which had a structure relevant to movement, and yet could not move. Thus, I sensed a void substituting in space the normal movement of my leg. The movement that my knee should have produced in space was now an experience of blankness that was held in space. In other words, my knee was destined to maintain a constant relationship with space, and through space it was intended to constantly be engaged in movement. The condition of my knee preserved the usual rapport between organ and space, but substituted

Appointments

In order to meet Jonathan one had to make an appointment. He was always very busy, and in order to meet friends, he had to cancel other activities. Sometimes a month or two would pass before we had an opportunity to meet Jonathan.

Shosh Foyerlicht

Each one is the only one in the world

Jonathan's household was complexed and multitasked – a giant team of assistants and caregivers, writers and artists – and everyone's schedule was run precisely and decisively by Jonathan with supernatural virtuoso. Jonathan ran this whole operation using his phone which he activated with one finger or his voice. When we wanted to meet with him out of longing – we had to make an appointment. But when we met, and even for a limited time, it was always with a warm welcome and joy. Jonathan always gave each person the feeling that he was the only one in the world. It was a wonderful feature.

Gadi Ravnitzki

the movement that should have been held in that space with a void that even felt as replacing the missing motion in that very same space. It was a void enveloped by space – by that space which my knee introduced to me. Thus my knee was opening up my awareness to an arena of space – space as a "container", which "contained" a void. Since this void was, of itself, an additional container (just like the void present in dreamless sleep). I found through my knee a "container" (void) held within another "container" (space). In this way disability provided me with a "container" within a "container"- a void completely embraced by space.

As I attempted to study my experience more in depth, I began to see that the main factor of my sensation was its dual nature. My knee was serving a double purpose in that, despite its being a single bodily element, it was introducing to me two distinct dimensions, each of a very different kind. An experience of both void and space, although radically different from each other, were simultaneously produced by a solitary element – my knee. Because of its direct connection to my calf and my thigh, my knee could not detach itself from the space dimension. My thigh had maintained its own individual spatial design which was different from that of my calf, and my knee had been exposed to a constant flow of experience, coming to it from these two distinct spatial elements. As a result, the space dimension was preserved in my knee through the separate inputs of my thigh and my calf. For me, therefore, knee and space were inseparable – I could not even conceive of my knee without having a sense of space. Because of my malady the presence of my calf and thigh was completely fixed in space. As a result their existence as spatial entities

Apple-pie order

The order in Jonathan's room was exemplary. In his little room there were hundreds of books and tapes, envelopes, papers and bills. Jonathan was familiar with the place of everything without seeing it. Who ever helped him to arrange a book, tape or paper received precise instructions on where to put it or where to take it out of. Nothing ever got lost and everything was easily found.

Uri Nissel

Jonathan's bookshelf

became even more pronounced. This in itself allowed an even more comprehensive sense of space to be infused into my knee. However, this very same fact, that my leg was paralyzed – brought with it an additional dimension which was almost diametrically opposed to that of space. Whenever I experience my knee I found that it was equally inseparable from the very same presence of my calf and my thigh.

Had I not been a disabled person, I believe I would have felt that the very nature of my knee, as such, was contingent rather than independent. Had I not been disabled my experience would have been that the existence of my knee as a knee was contingent upon movement in my calf and in my thigh. Had my body been "normal" it would have given me the impression that without such movement my knee could no longer serve as a joint. As a result of losing its characteristics as a joint it would also lose its knee identity. However, being disabled, my knee provided me with a sense of non-dependence on movement. It continued to be a knee – indeed, to be one of the only two knees I had – despite the fact that it was no longer serving as what is usually thought to be a "joint". My knee's nature was completely dependent upon something other than movement. Being paralyzed, my knee's nature seemed to depend upon the presence of void, both in my calf and in my thigh. My knee could exist as a knee only in so far as it would involve itself in the void-reality that both my calf and my thigh presented to it. Because of my knee's complete emergence in void an almost paradoxical state of affairs was established. As I've already mentioned, parallel to its involvement in void, my knee was equally absorbed

Technical advice

Jonathan knew how to utilize each of us to help him, in the way that suited us best. And so I found myself assembeling different integrated systems for him – radio speakers, amplifiers,video,TV – all with a special remote control and wires inside the cabinet and behind and along the walls of the room. Even though he had no technical knowledge himself, he knew exactly what he wanted, how he wanted it to be assembled and the systems capabilities and features. He always had ideas and advice on how to overcome difficulties and solve problems – leaveing me surprised and astonished.

Gadi Ravnitzki

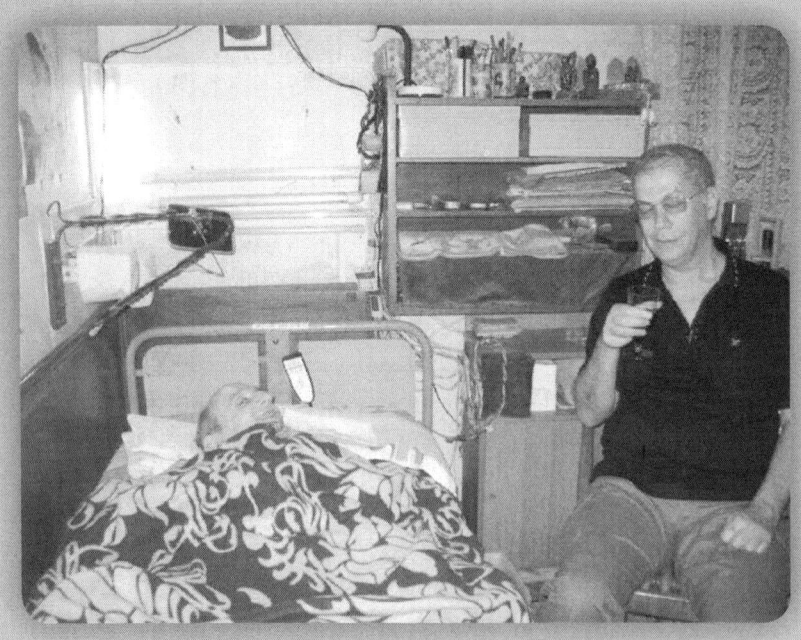

Haim Yechimovitz at the bedside of Jonathan
on his sixtieth birthday

in space. Although I genuinely experienced my knee as thoroughly soaked in both textures of void and space, my mind found great difficulty in trying to make sense of this fact. Void and space were viewed by my mind as contrary to each other – the void was the arena of things that did not exist in space, whereas space was the arena of things that did not exist in the void. Consequently my mind could not explain to itself what the nature of my knee truly was. Was my knee a space-entity or was it a void-entity? Were my knee a void-entity, in what way could it involve itself in the spatial nature of my calf and my thigh? On the other hand, were my knee a space-entity, how come it opened itself to the void emerging from the paralysis of my entire leg? These enigmas seemed to be insoluble. Yet the undeniable reality was that my knee was embracing both void and space. This state of affairs was a hard fact – actually it was as hard as any fact could be.

I was looking to my knee for answers to my inquiries. I felt that my paralyzed knee had gathered much information about the nature of void and space. It then transmitted this information to me. However, all this information streamed to me in a nonverbal form. It came from my knee in the form of sensations, impressions, and shades of inarticulate experiences. I could not put into words the content of what was coming my way, so that I attempted instead to invent an imaginary dialogue.

Payments

Paying Jonathan's caregivers was handeled in a special way. A friend would convert checks to cash. The money was then put into envelopes which were then hidden in a secret places under Jonathan's guidance. Each caregiver would receive his payment directly from Jonathan from a hiding place. Jonathan had absolute control.

Uri Nissel

Jonathan's house, 2013

CHAPTER 6

Personal Understanding

I conjured up a conversation that took place between my knee (as representing my disability), my eyes (which represented my non-disabled aspect), and finally my personal understanding (which bound together both my disabled and able aspects). The conversation began with my paralyzed knee addressing my personal understanding. My paralyzed knee came up with a complete speech, which began in the following way:

"The direction in which you tried to pursue your investigation is wrong. You have a narrow perspective of what space is and therefore the questions that you have raised are of very little significance. From my point of view, as a paralyzed knee, I must tell you that you are completely captivated by the perspective offered to you by your eyes. I would even go so far as to say that your whole notion of space is limited by what "meets your eye". Your eyes disclose to you the presence of space as an unbound arena. Whenever you view space what you see is a realm that

Loving and receiving love

I met John when I was in my 20s. I had just had my first my footsteps in the world as an adult, and Jonathan accompanied me during the years in which I studied, started a family, had children, painted and worked. I moved a lot, and Jonathan was always steady in place just as the Sun. Jonathan taught me the motion method he had developed. We went for long walks with him in the wheelchair, sat in cafes and talked and talked and we were friends. I had many questions about the world, and Jonathan listened and responded. Jonathan explained his theory on disability, and I listened and talked. We observed art together and discussed it. We listened to music together, and we talked. We rememberd each other's birthdays, celabrated the day together, giving love and attention, and we talked. Johnathan taught me to stop, to listen, to observe, to give things the time they needed. Disability allowed him to be like a mountain based strongly in the ground and its head in the clouds, birds and butterflies circling around it, on this mountain flowers and trees grow – and the mountain watches all the surroundings loving them all and reciving love.

Rinat Podissok Reisner

appears to you to be completely open. You, being a mere mind, cannot even conceive of the idea of the edge of space, let alone have any real image of it."

My eyes immediately responded to the accusations made by my paralyzed knee and answered in alarm:

"What are you saying here? Is it not obvious that space is the greatest "openness" to exist in the world? Is it not the case that the limits of space cannot be seen because they simply do not exist? Space itself has no restrictions whatsoever. However much you follow space, it will never stop introducing you to an ever-growing abundance of space. It just goes on and on in all directions and this is precisely what we let you see when we scan it. Look around you as we do and you'll see for yourself."

It became apparent that a huge gap separated the opinions held by my paralyzed knee from those held by my seeing eyes. As a result my personal understanding went into a state of utter shock. It protested:

"Both of you, knee and eyes are parts of the very same system. It doesn't make any sense to me – I would even say that it appears illogical and irrational – that you should disagree among yourselves. It doesn't make any sense to me that a unified system, like the one in which you and I exist, will in some aspects disagree with itself. In short, I believe that we should all work together, towards having the same world view. Therefore, I suggest that you continue your exchange of opinions until you find a way of agreeing in what you believe to be true. My promise to – the knee and the eyes of my system – is to assist you as much as I can in coming to such a common understanding. So, let's take the journey together, working towards a shared

Sixtieth birthday, sitting at his bedside his mother Anna,
Noga and Lior

comprehension that will surpass those that each of you now hold. Such a shared comprehension will go beyond the perspective of movement and stillness, non-disability and paralysis."

My paralyzed knee responded by saying:

"I think that having the very dialogue we are now sharing is aimed at the purpose you have just defined. I would like to share with both of you – the eyes of my system and its personal understanding – my own experiences so that what I feel and sense will be accessible not only to me, but equally to all of us."

"What I sense and feel" continued my paralyzed knee "is that, if space were to lead only to more space, then indeed, nothing other than itself would be accessible to space. My experience, however, is that, as opposed to being enclosed within itself, space is open everywhere and always. The difficulty is that what space opens up to is only one thing – a void. Since a void, by its very definition, holds nothing that is three-dimensional (a void is not spatial in any way) it cannot be easily recognized. So that space opens up everywhere and always to something that can hardly at all be recognized. Luckily, there exists a special occasion where the opening up of space to the void becomes recognizable to most creatures – this includes our own species, mankind. This special occasion is present as each person wakes up or falls asleep. As one falls asleep, one can track down that point which fuses space (the world that extends all around) with the void (dreamless sleep). It is not accidental that one can fall asleep in almost any place and at almost any moment. Whether one has put to use this fact in falling asleep or not, the case remains the same;

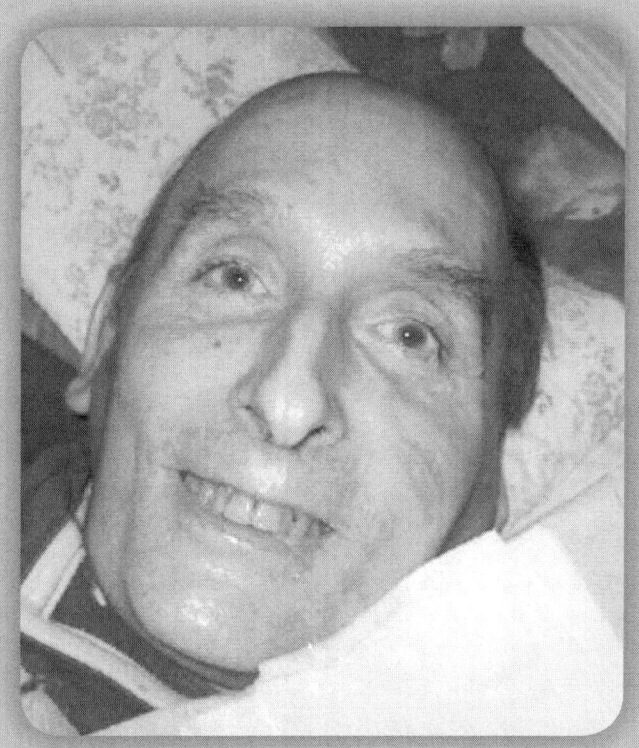

Noga's kiss (lipstick on the cheek)on his sixtieth birthday

space opens up everywhere and always to the void. When we do indeed fall asleep, we are also capable of recognizing this fact, but when we do not fall asleep the fact remains the same, without us recognizing it."

My personal understanding seemed stimulated by what my paralyzed leg had said. My personal understanding then turned to my leg and asked it:

"Could you give a more personal account of what you feel when crossing the threshold between space and the void? You see, I exist as a personal understanding, and being so, I have a better understanding only of those things which are presented to me in a personal way. What is personal appeals to me and what is not personal does not." My paralyzed leg immediately protested:

"But what you are claiming to be is a capacity to understand. Why should you not be able to understand something that is not personal". My opinion is that for anything to be fully understood it must be both personal and impersonal. In order to clarify this point, I would like to give an account of the subject we are discussing not from my point of view, but instead from the point of view of a scientific theory. I am asking myself," said my paralyzed leg, "how the subject under discussion would be viewed, say, by Darwinian thinking. I hope that by using Darwinian concepts, I'll be able to give you an impersonal description of the threshold that exists between space and the void."

"How very strange," replied my eyes, "you, and specifically you, want to give us an impersonal description – but this seems a contradiction in terms – we are all personal entities discussing with each other. How can anything coming

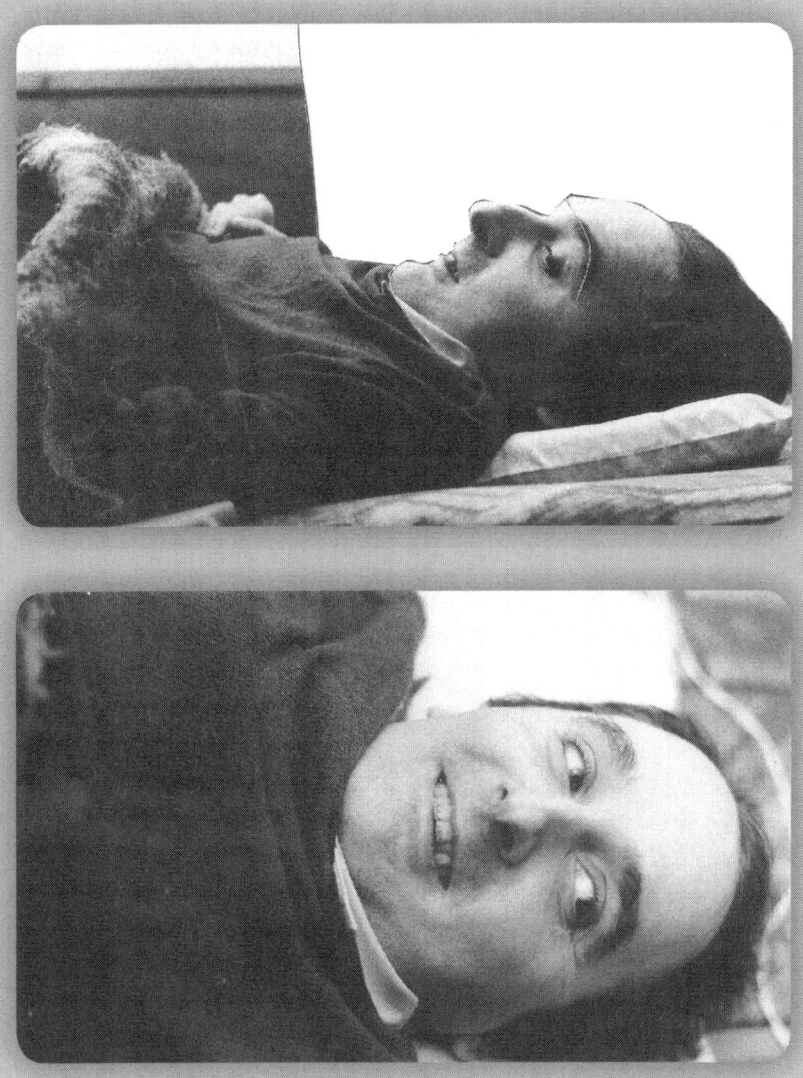

Dan Reisner's photo of making the statue of Jonathan

from you be impersonal? Anything you say will be your personal expression." To this my paralyzed leg replied:

"Are the three of us, indeed, personal entities? I do not think so. At the very most, all three of us belong to a personal organism of which we are only parts. Therefore, I insist upon turning to Darwinian concepts since they treat the evolution of the entire species not only from a personal point of view, but also from a general, impersonal perspective."

"I am not sure that I understand you," said my personal understanding, "despite my being a personal understanding. I would like, however, to try and understand what you mean, so please try us out and give us your description."

"Well," said my paralyzed leg, "I will at least try to do so. According to Darwin, those organisms that have survived natural selection are the fittest. Now, we know that through this process the most extraordinary inventions have been produced in nature, Almost unthinkable symbiotic relations between different systems, the strangest combination of functions, and the most peculiar shapes of organs can be found almost everywhere and on just about every level of existence. These outcomes of natural selection seem to fit their environments in the most efficient way. However, what seems to be problematic," explained my paralyzed leg, "is the fact that so many of these organisms waste so much of the time they have in sleep. Sleep can be regarded not only as an absence of vigilance, which could prove crucial to the very existence of the creature, but it also places the creature in a dangerous position as a possible victim of other hunters. Thus sleep appears to me as the least efficient mode in which any creature would exist.

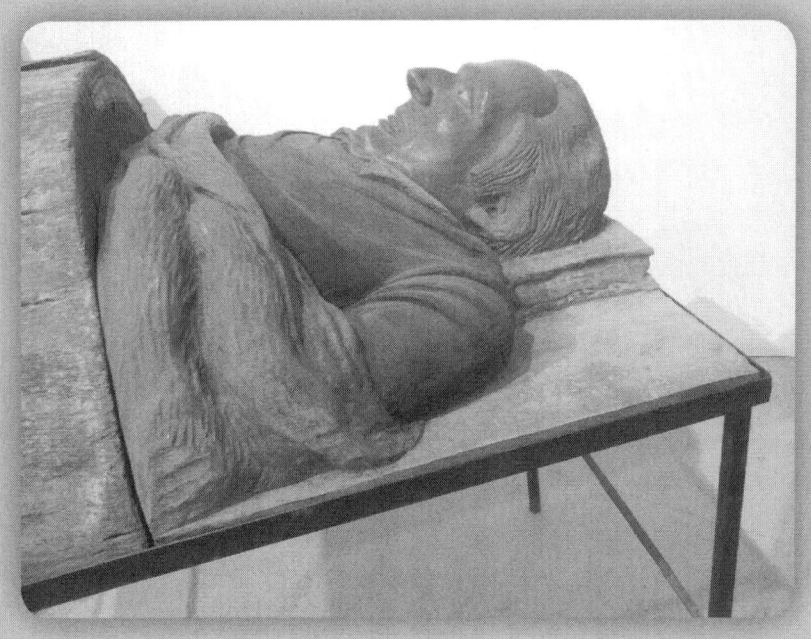

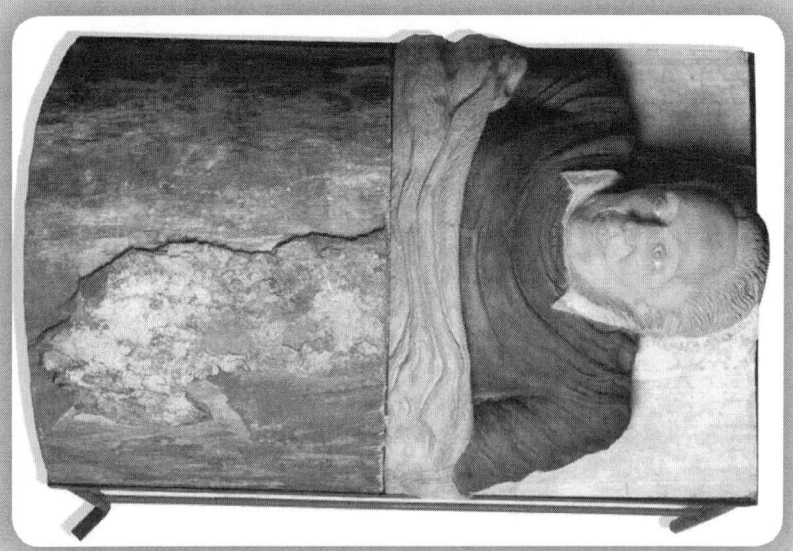

The statue sculpted by Dan Reisner

In short, at first glance sleep seems to have been quite an unhappy invention. Moreover, how come that nature, after having found solutions to the most complex difficulties that arose in the course of evolution, could not find a solution to sleep. After all, it has invented creatures which can run, swim, fly, or do several if not all of these feats and much more. How come it did not invent a creature which was vigilant and mobile whilst sleeping?"

"That's just it," replied my personal understanding. "You have pronounced your speech eloquently, unraveling some very broad and general ideas. I'm afraid, however, that nothing in your words has in any way affected me. I see what you are trying to point at – the inefficiency of sleep in the context of a competing world of creatures, which are struggling to survive. But why should I care about such abstract concepts and indeed, why should you care? You are, after all, a paralyzed leg, and as such, I doubt that you could even participate in such a contest and emerge on the winning side – alive. So in what way could you picture yourself as belonging in the image of nature you conjured up for us? Why do you find Darwin's theory relevant at all, to either your condition or ours?"

"The idea I was trying to put across," said my paralyzed leg, "was a conviction I hold on to. I believe that each and every creature on the face of the earth – whether it swims, flies, leaps, crawls, walks, etc. – regularly needs to enter the sleeping condition and to emerge from it only after having been in it for a good while. Most creatures in the biological world stay in the void for quite a remarkable portion of their lives. They unavoidably plunge into sleep – this world of darkness which could be coined "a no-man's

Beauty and Joy

My last meeting with him shortly before his death was different from all our meetings in the past. As if he knew we shall not see each other again, he concluded with stunning accuracy the long history we've been through together from the time he was a boy. Suddenly we became two equal adults who share the life they had when they were together.

I remembered our first meeting just as he did. How Moshe Feldenkrais one day in the fifties took me to the apartment on Bnei Moshe Street. The door opened and Jonathan's mother Annie stood on the threshold, her wonderful eyes light up and next in a wheelchair sat Jonathan, his face shining and beautiful like his mother. This was my first time to meet with a child so disabled. But at that moment I did not realize his situation, because I was riveted from the first moment to the beauty and joy radiating around them.

From that day I witnessed all the lessons Moses gave Jonathan. It was not long and I was also guiding him, and the relationship with him and his mother was beyond treatment – warm, personal and close. I met his friends. They loved and admired him. Jonathan was brimming with optimism and knowledge. With Benny and Leon he spoke among other things about basketball as if he was playing basketball. With my daughter Leora he had long talks about music and art, and one could think this was what he did.

By profession I meet many people who are suffering pain or feel that their lives are not good. But many times I say to myself that the healthiest man I know is lying in his room, unable to move, getting weaker physically, but lives a full life, learning and teaching, creating and enriching himself and those around him.

When we finished a lesson, Annie joined our conversations. This noble and wonderful woman was a heroine and designer through which Jonathan experienced the world. In their small apartment land", since most of humanity does not want to admit the existence of the void. However, most creatures in nature appear to admit the presence of the void and even to value its significance. It can be seen by merely observing the creatures' behavior, that the void is very highly regarded by them. As I am about to explain, in order to obtain a place in the void, these creatures are ready to strive and struggle for it in a variety of ways during their waking hours, and then put their lives in jeopardy when sleeping. Most, if not all creatures, spend much time in the void – in sleep, a time that could have been otherwise used for hunting, but which they spend in a way that often puts their lives at risk (other creatures can easily hunt them during that period). However, many of these creatures not only devote much time to the void when sleeping takes place, but find it reasonable to find even more time during their waking hours for the purpose of preparing for sleep. Some of them dig holes, others look around for empty caves, and yet others even go as far as exploring the higher branches of trees in order to find sleeping accommodation (such as nests). All of this activity is aimed at securing the best possible place for sleeping – for entering the void."

My personal understanding put on an almost angry expression:

"In what way do all of these dry facts concern me? Why should I, you, or anyone else be interested in the way in which rats and grasshoppers spend their sleeping time? I think we should be concerned with issues in which we are far more involved."

There is hardly anything that more involves all the aspects of my existence than the sleeping habits of the creatures she opened windows from which came not only studies and knowledge. There was a lot of love and moral values and mutual respect honesty and dedication without reservation.

Actually I got there thanks to his body. This mall body, brave and loyal which, despite the enormous difficulties could for sixty years feel, see and hear and think and live. I came to help him. I experienced with Jonathan days of the mise ry and days of happiness, and I was a witness when he flew up to wonderful human levels.

Some people come into my world and enrich it, and in difficult times I can remember the light of their face and understand how wonderful was our meeting. Jonathan was for me a man like that. And I am grateful for this gift.

Mia Segal

I have just described." replied my paralyzed leg. "These creatures are exploring the world during their waking state – when preparing for the night in order to detect rare parts of reality where a profound stillness prevails. The soil that would be trodden under me, were I not paralyzed" continued my paralyzed leg, "can be regarded as the epitome of quietude. Unless there is an earthquake, a hole in the ground remains as unmoving as anything can be – it is as unchanging as a cave. These creatures evaluate the peacefulness of a cave in a mountain or the stillness of a hole in the ground as being enormously precious, precisely because of the profound quietude that both cave and hole hold as inherent to them. What these creatures discover in the ground, in a mountain or on the branch of an old majestic tree is a gateway in space – a point in space where space opens up to another dimension: the void. What they are looking for in their waking state and indeed what they eventually find in sleep, are parts of the world where space seems to transform itself easily into the void."

"How strange," asserted my eyes. "From what you said one could truly believe that the whole world of nature – at least all the animal kingdom – is very much sensitive to the presence of the void. This whole approach of yours seems to us unacceptable. Although we are a pair of eyes who look at the world almost constantly, we have never, as a matter of fact, detected the void nor did we ever feel any need to be sensitive to it. What explanation could you give for that?"

"To be honest with you," responded my paralyzed leg, "I believe that despite the fact that you exist as a pair of eyes, to me you are quite blind: You do not appear to see

Layers of Personality

There's no phrase more apt than "The Human Within Us" to describe Yonatan and the many layers of his personality. For over ten years we have worked together once a week. Working together means that one person gives of his knowledge and a conversation is created – sometimes in words, and sometimes without them. Moshe Feldenkrais called it a tango for two. One leading, the other following, but the dance is for two.

The reason for our meetings was to allow Yonatan's joints and organs to perform a movement which he could not perform himself, and through this reach awareness. This movement gradually decreased over the years.

At the same time, Yonatan was able to lead me to places where he wanted to change position, touch, and receive support from a pillow or my hands. Though part of his body was paralyzed, it was surprising to see his understanding of the motor system which requires insight and self awareness.

For one of our meetings I brought a thin wooden plank with me, to create a sort of artificial floor for his foot to simulate the experience of walking. Thus, gently and with small movements, we began the conversation between the foot and the simulation of the function of standing or walking. My intent was to give his mind the sensation with which a child feels the floor with his first steps, and through the sole he can adjust his foot to the changing characteristics of the ground. For Yonatan it felt like an experience of standing, though it was all done with him lying on his back. Nothing is taken for granted for someone who had never stood or taken a step on his feet by himself and without support for years.

At each of our meetings Yonatan inspired me and I felt that I was transcending daily life. The meeting between us became a sacred Sabbath. The conversations we had during the lessons were peppered with his proficiency in a variety of fields and with those things which my whole existence revolves around. I therefore suggest that we look together into this whole issue, so that both you and I will catch a better glimpse of the world in its fullness."

"How atrocious," protested my eyes, "you mean to say that we are incapable of seeing something that every lizard, snail or bug is in touch with?"

"Very much so," said my paralyzed leg. "Moreover, I believe that were we to go 'down' the evolutionary ladder and enter the plant world we would be facing the inescapable fact that any flower perceives reality in a way that is far more refined than yours."

"How dare you say such a thing!" said my eyes, which were by then in a state of complete shock.

At this point my paralyzed leg began a new discourse:

"Everyone can see how space forms the dimension in which the physical world exists. However, the blossoming of a flower shows us a broader perspective of the way in which things stand. Latent aspects of the world around us are revealed to us as a flower blossoms in its own stillness. Were we to ignore the blossoming of a flower, we would be trapped in a belief that being a plant exists only in space. However, as we perceive the entire scope of blossoming the very same flower would no longer appear to be captured in space. By the sheer power of its stillness the flower gives the impression that it is finding a way of its own to reach beyond space. A flower is a creature that bursts the boundaries of space in order to enter an additional domain – the void. The blossoming of petals allows the borders of space to be transgressed, in a way which makes obvious the fact that the void's stillness is not of space.

philosophical conversation that enriched my life with philosophical understanding and knowledge, or with music and art. I was surprised anew every time, to get to know the man who knew the world though he never stepped past the threshold of his home.

In those years I conducted a course for training teachers in the Feldenkrais method, and Yonatan wanted to come to visit and lecture the class. He wanted to share his experiences with the students, share his knowledge of the system and Moshe Feldenkrais, and tell them of how the method had contributed to his life and his own understanding of the method.

Over the years I discovered that following these meetings with the course's students, several students gathered around Yonatan who were interested in continuing to meet with him. Some of them continued visiting him individually and assisted him in writing his thoughts and ideas. Other continued visiting him at his home and reported of the great contribution Yonatan had given them. Like me, they felt that they got a lot more than what they gave.

Throughout the years, Yonatan expressed an interest in my family, my studies, the children's occupations, and even when we didn't met we held long and in-depth telephone conversations which continued to echo in my mind long after they were over.

Chava Shelhav

The void, when brought forth by a flower, is a presence whose beauty cannot be traveled through mechanically – it cannot be entered, traversed, or exited by movement. When one studies the world through the stillness of plant vitality one can clearly see that in no way can movement touch the unmoving reality of the void."

"Frankly, we do not know what you're talking about," said my eyes. "We certainly cannot see a void, either when we look directly into space or when we view it through the figure of a flower. What sounds most unconvincing to us in your words is your insistence that a paralyzed leg like yourself, whose existence is not aimed at seeing a thing, should have the pretension to see things that we cannot see." My personal understanding joined in, with a similar criticism of what my paralyzed leg tried to express.

"What you call 'the void' sounds like an empty word – a word that doesn't signify a thing. For me," said my personal understanding, "what you have done is simply to invent a meaningless word – a word that does not represent anything real. Once and for all, could you please at least try to give a somewhat clear definition of what 'the void' is?" My paralyzed leg met the challenge in the following way:

"Concerning the void, you should not be surprised that I have such a vivid experience of it. My whole existence resides exclusively in the void because of my being almost completely still. The stillness of my paralysis provides for a total acquaintance with the very heart of the void. For most of my life I have been in touch with nothing other than the void – I have "seen" nothing other than the void, "heard" nothing other than the void. I have lived most of my life in the hues of the void's various "tastes", "smells",

Movement is life
Without Movement life is
unthinkable —

Moshe Feldenkrais

and every other impression that it can produce. This puts me in a position to give, I believe, an adequate account of the void's nature.

"Regarding your question of whether the void exists at all," my paralyzed leg went on, "I have this to say. Whenever one has an emotion of any kind (and that includes you – the eyes, and you – the personal understanding), then at that very moment, one is making use of the void. The void is the facility which serves to hold all the emotions that exist in the world. The world consists, among other things, of a huge variety of emotions, all of which can only be contained in the void. I believe that each one of us ought to inquire as to where one's emotions go once one has produced them. It must be very obvious to you that, once you have produced a movement, that movement will unavoidably go into space – it cannot do otherwise than work its way through space. When you move any part of your body (e.g. wave your hand) only space can contain this action. A similar thing is undoubtedly taking place with your thoughts. Once you've produced a thought it will unquestionably exist within your mind – every thought that you have will direct itself to occupy a certain part of your mental activity. Thus, you know that every movement goes into space and every thought goes into the mind. Did you ever ask yourself where your emotions went? They certainly do not go into space since you can never find them there. The emotions that you have do not belong in your mind – unless you mistake your emotions for thoughts. It is quite obvious that a mind cannot "feel" – it can "think", and therefore thoughts can be found in the mind. But where should your emotions be looked for? – In space? – I doubt it! – In your mind? – I doubt it just as much!"

"For once, your words make some sense to me," commented my personal understanding. "I will admit that I perceive movement through space and that I perceive thoughts through the mind. But I cannot see that anything else exists except the mind (that is, myself) and space (that is, the world). So, again, what do you mean when you mention "the void", and how is one to perceive it?"

At this point, for the first time, a difference of opinion arose between my personal understanding and my eyes. My eyes said: "We have very often seen movements that were going into space. However, your comparison" (by 'your' they meant my paralyzed leg) "of space and mind seems inappropriate to us. In fact, we have never seen a thought go into the mind. Actually, a thought is not visible and therefore it doesn't make any sense to us that a thought could be seen as going or not going into anything at all." The debate warmed up as my personal understanding commented:

"I don't care what eyes can see or cannot see. From my part, I constantly see thoughts through the mind's eye and they are always directed straight into the mind."

Here, my paralyzed leg spoke for the first time in irony:

"I'm afraid that just as the Personal Understanding could consider the eyes as being completely blind to mental processes, I would consider the Personal Understanding at least for the time being to be completely blind to the presence of the void. In order to clarify the point I am trying to make," continued my paralyzed leg, "I would like to compare the world of emotion (with its void) to the world of sight (with its eyes and the complete panorama which they are seeing). My claim is that like the world of sight, which revolves around an organ – the eyes – so the void is a world in itself, which must revolve around an organ – the emotion. When the faculty of seeing matures, it recognized itself as acting as an independent organ – the eye – which functions within an autonomous world – the world of shapes, colors, proportions, etc. – in short, the visual world. Similarly, when the world of emotion reaches full maturity, it too becomes an organ (like the eye), capable of recognizing an independent world in which it functions. Therefore, we can say that the world of emotion must be developed to a point where it becomes a self-reliant agent, which acts as an independent organ. The world of emotion must be powerful and self-aware to a degree where it can recognize itself as an autonomous faculty working its way into its own arena – the void. Only then, when they indeed become an organ, will the emotions perceive the "arena" in which they operate (the void) as having a self-sufficient existence. In short, in order to "see" the "void", one must be able to "feel" its presence. The only way to "feel" it is through the very existence of the world of emotion itself."

Again my eyes seemed to want to involve themselves in the discussion:

"Assuming that what you are saying has real meaning to It, and that an emotional equivalent to us could in fact exist, we would coin such a correlative organ "The Emotional Eye".

"A name appropriately given," said my personal understanding in good cheer. Since my paralyzed leg seemed similarly happy with the new name, the three debaters soon accepted it. Being so successful in this attempt, my eyes carried on with their argument: "You called us 'blind' when considering the mind and its thoughts, and yet you accepted us as the most reliable authority on the whole issue of seeing into space. We can thus tell you, with full authority, that anything that can be seen in space can be seen and exist inside space – as part of space. Although we cannot see thoughts neither can we see the mind (in the way that the Personal Understanding claims to do), we gather that thoughts, when seen by the mind's eye, appear inside the mind. Now you, who claim to be an authority on the issue of "The Emotional Eye" (my eyes were addressing my paralyzed leg), tell us more about the way in which the void can be seen. Does the void appear inside of space and as part of space when it is seen by "The Emotional Eye", or does it appear outside of space – as in the case of thoughts which according to you, can be seen in the mind? Since we do not possess a faculty that can see into the mind, but we do possess the only faculty that can see into space, we would be interested in your clarifying for us the entire issue of the relationship between void and space (space being our natural domain)."

"Sometimes the void is inside space, and sometimes space is inside the void," responded my paralyzed leg. "When the void is inside space, it becomes part of space – almost a spatial entity. Then, as a result, the void acts according to the rules that mold space. The void, thus, breaks up into different compartments, each occupying a specific location. Space would, in such a case, be comprised of numerous voids, each of which exists in its special place. This happens when we are awake, when we live in the "real" world. In those portions of space where the void prevails, the world virtually takes on a magical semblance. This can be experienced when one is touring a garden or a park. In such locations, space appears to be full of spatial entities: trees, bushes, flowers, and endless numbers of blades of grass. In truth, however, one does not experience these entities only as space-bound. Each is rooted both in its own place and also in its own stillness – in its own void. Belonging to the plant kingdom all plants have an inherent stillness to them – they all abstain from moving in space. The "magic" of a garden is brought about because of this structured stillness. One walks – one moves through the space of a garden – whilst on all sides there exist living plants that do not move in space, but rather produce a great ambience of stillness. One may say, and indeed not only say, but also feel very deeply that the stillness of such a park is structured spatially. On the one hand, the part as a whole holds an immense quietude, which by its very nature cannot be divided into different parts (Stillness is always total because of its natural complete unity). Yet, on the other hand, one is capable of detecting specific compartments of stillness as one tours the park. It is very clear that each tree and each flower has its own special domain in which a unique stillness prevails. Thus, one can realize, when visiting a garden, what I have already claimed – that space would, in such a case, be comprised of numerous voids, each of which exists in its spatial space.

It also happens that one can find a "chunk" of space contained within the void. On such occasions, when space is "captured" in a void-like environment, space becomes part of the void. Space is then transformed into a void-like entity. This happens when we dream in our sleep, when we live in the dream world. A dream takes place in space: a dream is a series of events, which had a space-like appearance. However, the space of a dream is not an ordinary space. It is a space whose rules do not belong to space, as such. Instead, the rules that dominate any dream-space are derived from the reality of the void, inside of which such a dream-space can thus be likened to a strange "magic box". It is a "dark chamber" in which all the photographs, which are developed, do not represent space, but stand out instead as images of the void. Each such image, which on the outside seems as the dreamer's way of envisioning space, does in truth express the inner rules of the void. Now, as we saw, a void is a container of emotions. It is a container which acts according to emotional patterns. Thus, a dream becomes a space that is guided by a set of rules, which would not normally mold the form of space, but instead, would fashion the pattern of the emotional domain (the void dimension). A dream cannot occur unless what takes place through it is a series of genuine emotions. The events of a dream are so packed with emotions that their very location in the dream's plot reveal an emotional plan. Thus, in a dream, space follows a pattern, which is almost unreal, as each event of the dream no longer fits its specific location, but instead fits a unique motion. It could even be said that in the case of a dream the reality of the emotions (i.e. the way in which the void exists) fabricates the world of every day facts (i.e. the reality which exists in space). Thus the purpose of a dream is to allow the dreamer's emotions to bring into existence a spatial world. Consequently the spatial aspect of a dream serves as evidence to the fact that the dreamer exists as an integral part of the void. In short, dreaming manifests the truth that the dreamer's emotions (his void aspect) can produce "hard facts" (his space aspect).

"What you said about the world of a dream has some meaning for me," commented my personal understanding. "However, the way in which you described a garden as containing voids within its space – that seems completely obscure." My paralyzed leg, after some thought, gave the following answer:

"When you said that my description of the mystery of a dream had some sense for you, why did you say so? What was it in my description that sounded familiar to you? Was there anything there that you had already experienced for yourself?" My personal understanding responded:

"Well, I have often recognized – actually I've been doing it every single night – that dreams do indeed take place in a special space. As you said, the space that exists in a dream has something very unusual to it. It is a space loaded with exceptionally intense emotions."

"But how do you know this? How did you arrive at this conclusion? I mean, what made you realize that a dream holds a special space?" inquired my paralyzed leg.

"Well, I feel it to be so," responded my personal understanding. "When I'm facing a dream I cannot but have a very strong impression that what lies in front of me produces a very unusual kind of atmosphere."

"But that is exactly it," answered my paralyzed leg. "One needs to feel, and one can only feel one's way to the void whenever one is about to detect it." (My paralyzed leg emphasized the word 'feel' the first two times it used the word). "As you yourself admitted you can only feel (my paralyzed leg again emphasized the word 'feel') that the void is in your immediate environment when dreaming. You called the impact of the void 'a special space' which you feel when dreaming. It is true that the space of a dream has a very unique texture to it, which makes it outstanding. But this uniqueness – these outstanding textures – are the result of your capacity to feel through the space of a dream and reach what lies beyond it – the void. When you stop dreaming and remain asleep – in a state of dreamless sleep, you can realize, that the space of the dream that you had before was enveloped by sleep – by a blankness, or a nothingness which in truth is a void. It is this void that you feel throughout your dream as something unusual you feel this void in the unique ambiance that molds the space in which the dream happens. To conclude this speech of mine, what I have been trying to say is that it is the void which is continually enveloping each single episode of the dream. In short, I hope you understood by now that only this enveloping void can refashion the dream's space."

"But where do you know all of this from?" asked my personal understanding. "Any dreamer is aware only of the space in which the dream happens. You should try to ask the other organs that constitute the person you are part of, about their dreaming experience when the whole person is asleep," continued my personal understanding when addressing my paralyzed leg. "You would find out that when dreaming the non-paralyzed organs can perceive only that spatial arena where the plot of the dream takes place – they only perceive the dreams' inner space. When you were speaking about dreams you were describing them as if you could perceive something that other sleeping organs cannot perceive: the void that lies beyond the space of a dream. In so doing you attributed to yourself a talent which no other dreamer normally enjoys – the talent to transcend space and enter the void. What allows you to be so presumptuous as to set yourself up as an authority on such issues?"

"That is a question that I can easily answer", replied my paralyzed leg. "It is precisely my being paralyzed that takes me away from the normal orientation that any moving organ has. Any moving organ must confine its movement to spatial boundaries. However since I do not move I am not compelled to narrow my repertoire to the arena of motion – to space. Quite the opposite, being immobile I am capable of transcending that context to which movement is confined. I have the ability to transcend the confines of space. It is, to be more specific, my motionless state that puts me in the privileged position of relating intensely to the world of the void.

"I would like you to be clear about what it is that you are claiming," uttered my personal understanding, sounding doubtful. "Are you trying to indicate that your inert condition produces in you a rare sensitivity to both space and what you argue is beyond it – the void?"

"I would certainly like to be as clear as I can on this issue. Moreover, I would be very happy if both you and I were to be as clear about it as we, two can possibly be," replied my paralyzed leg. "We both should bear in mind that when we are considering a dream (that is, a space enveloped by a void) we are concerned with a moving system – the human body. In other words, we are concerned with a system whose very nature – its movement – belongs solely to space, but which is at rest now, when sleeping. Without space there can be no movement, and indeed, the events of a dream need a space in which they can occur. Hence a dream, by its very nature, reflects the dreamer as a moving creature – a creature that can perceive itself only in space. However, if that were the whole story, I don't think it would be stimulating in any way and I don't think it would have anything to do with my own condition – with my paralysis. But the account I have so far given of a dream is not complete. Actually I have purposely omitted what is perhaps the most significant aspect of dreaming. I mean by that, that the dreamer I have so far described has an organism whose purpose is to move – an organism which was meant to walk, run, jump, etc. Strangely enough, when sleeping that organism resembles me – a paralyzed leg. I too was meant to walk, jump, run, etc., but instead, I maintained the highest degree of stillness possible for a limb such as myself. Like a dreamer, who is asleep and who abstains from most of the possible movements in space, I too maintain my quietude within the bounds of space. Therefore you should realize that both a dreamer and myself, a paralyzed leg, could not evade space. We might explore through our stillness more profound meanings than those that exist in space. However even those meanings that exceed anything that can be found in space, are made accessible to us through space, and through space alone.

You can see for yourself that every sleeping person when dreaming, can conceive only a dream that takes place in space (and therefore dreams must appear as being real – as happening in a spatial reality). For instance, one can dream of a dog chasing a cat, and although both the chasing dog and the chased cat are only dreamt and therefore do not exist in the real world, they nevertheless appear to be as real as space itself. However the space in which a dream happens is at times a very unusual space – most things might happen in it in an "unreal" way – in a dreamlike way. For instance, one can dream of a dog which at first only chases a cat, but then quite unexpectedly turns into the cat that was chased. Such a dreamt dog has both the real quality that does not belong to the reality of a spatial creature – it turns into a cat. I too, because of my unmoving nature, live in an unusual space – in a space, which has both the quality of reality and the quality of something quite different. I therefore believe that I have a good understanding of a dreamer's world. Both the dreamer and myself not only maintain our own quietude in space, but also sense the relationship of space to something else that remolds it and gives it a deeper, more meaningful quality. I feel that when space is filtered, either through the dreaming condition or through my immobile state, it undergoes a correlative alteration. The reason why, in both cases, space is recreated – having to it a certain new "otherness" – is that something external to space is truly acting upon it. This transformation happens to space only as a result of its being subject to the effect of an external cause.

7563544R00115

Printed in Great Britain
by Amazon.co.uk, Ltd.,
Marston Gate.